maranGraphics'™

Learn at First Sight
MS-DOS® 6.0

**Ruth Maran and
Richard Maran**

**Distributed in United States
by Regents/Prentice Hall**

Telephone: 1-800-223-1360
Fax: 1-800-445-6991

**Distributed in Canada
by Prentice Hall Canada**

Telephone: 1-800-567-3800
Fax: 416-299-2529

**Distributed Internationally
by Simon & Schuster**

Telephone: 201-767-4990
Fax: 201-767-5625

SINGLE COPY PURCHASES

Telephone: 1-800-947-7700
Fax: 515-284-2607

maranGraphics'™ *Learn at First Sight* MS-DOS® 6.0

Copyright©   maranGraphics Inc., 1993
5755 Coopers Avenue
Mississauga, Ontario, Canada
L4Z 1R9

Screen shots reprinted with permission
from Microsoft Corporation.

Published 1993.

Library of Congress Cataloging-in-Publication Data

Maran, Ruth, 1970-
    MaranGraphics' simplified computer guide for Microsoft
MS-DOS 6.0 / Ruth Maran and Richard Maran.
        p.   cm.
    Includes index.
    ISBN 0-13-064650-4
    1. Operating systems (Computers) 2. MS-DOS
(Computer file) I. Maran, Richard. II. Title.
QA76.76.063M362 1993
005.4'469--dc20   93-7169
                                                    CIP

Trademark Acknowledgments

maranGraphics Inc. has attempted to include
trademark information for products, services and
companies referred to in this guide. Although
maranGraphics Inc. has made reasonable efforts
in gathering this information, it cannot guarantee
its accuracy.

Lotus and 1-2-3 are registered trademarks of Lotus
Development Corporation.

Defragmenter, Microsoft Anti-Virus, Microsoft and
MS-DOS are registered trademarks of Microsoft
Corporation.

The Microsoft Mouse design is a trademark of
Microsoft Corporation.

WordPerfect is a registered trademark of
WordPerfect Corporation.

Bernoulli is a registered trademark of Iomega
Corporation.

Cover Design and Art Director:
Jim C. Leung

Illustrator:
Dave Ross

Screen Production:
Béla Korcsog

Technical Consultant:
Eric Feistmantl

Editing:
Maria Damiano

Film generated on
maranGraphics'
Linotronic L-330
imagesetter at 2540 dpi
resolution.

Acknowledgments

To Ted Werthman of Regents/Prentice Hall for his assistance and creative input.

Special thanks to Alec Saunders and John Hodgins of Microsoft Canada Inc. and Marilyn Meyer for their support and consultation.

To the dedicated staff of maranGraphics, including Maria Damiano, Monica DeVries, Eric Feistmantl, Béla Korcsog, Jim C. Leung, Jill Maran, Maxine Maran, Robert Maran and Dave Ross.

Table of Contents

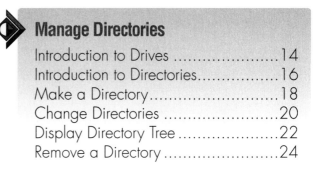

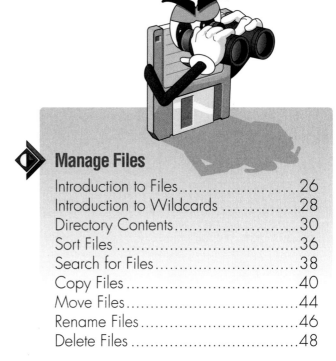

What is MS-DOS?

You can describe MS-DOS as your computer's master control program. Like a traffic cop, it keeps everything flowing smoothly.

A collection of programs makes up MS-DOS. They help you:

◆ Manage your files.

◆ Deal with peripheral devices such as your printer.

◆ Control and optimize your computer.

GETTING STARTED	MANAGE DIRECTORIES	MANAGE FILES	MANAGE DISKETTES	MS-DOS SHELL	BACKUP	DATA PROTECTION	DISK MANAGEMENT

INTRODUCTION
START MS-DOS
ENTER A COMMAND
DISPLAY VERSION NUMBER
CLEAR THE SCREEN
CHANGE DATE OR TIME
IMPORTANT KEYS
HELP

What MS-DOS Does

When you first turn on your computer, a small program checks all internal devices, electronic memory and peripherals to ensure they are functioning properly. Once it completes this test, MS-DOS is loaded.

◆ MS-DOS acts like a traffic cop. It enforces basic rules that all programs must follow.

Programs perform tasks such as word processing and spreadsheet analysis. MS-DOS controls how these programs input and output their data.

MS-DOS controls how a program interacts with you.

MS-DOS provides tools to store and organize files and to optimize your computer system.

1 Turn on your computer. It automatically performs a diagnostic check on itself. If the check is OK, the computer beeps once and displays either the **Command Prompt** (**C:\>**) or the **MS-DOS Shell** screen.

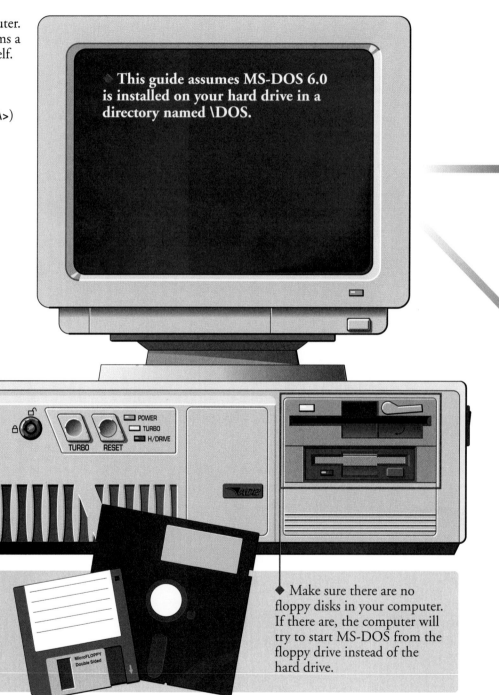

◆ This guide assumes MS-DOS 6.0 is installed on your hard drive in a directory named \DOS.

◆ Make sure there are no floppy disks in your computer. If there are, the computer will try to start MS-DOS from the floppy drive instead of the hard drive.

MicroFLOPPY
Double Sided

INTRODUCTION
START MS-DOS
ENTER A COMMAND
DISPLAY VERSION NUMBER
CLEAR THE SCREEN
CHANGE DATE OR TIME
IMPORTANT KEYS
HELP

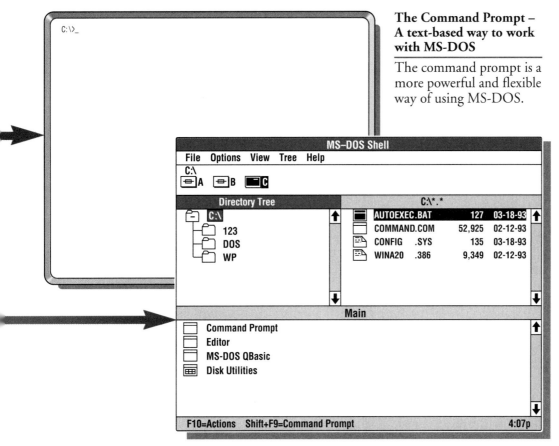

C:\>_

The Command Prompt – A text-based way to work with MS-DOS

The command prompt is a more powerful and flexible way of using MS-DOS.

The MS-DOS Shell – A graphic way to work with MS-DOS

The MS-DOS Shell provides an easy, graphic approach to using most MS-DOS commands.

◆ While installing MS-DOS, you were asked if you wanted to run the MS-DOS Shell on start-up.

If you chose **Yes**, the MS-DOS Shell screen appears when you turn on your computer.

If you want to display the command prompt **C:\>**, press **F3** to exit the MS-DOS Shell.

For more information on the MS-DOS Shell, see page 56.

5

Enter a Command

A command instructs MS-DOS to perform a specific task.

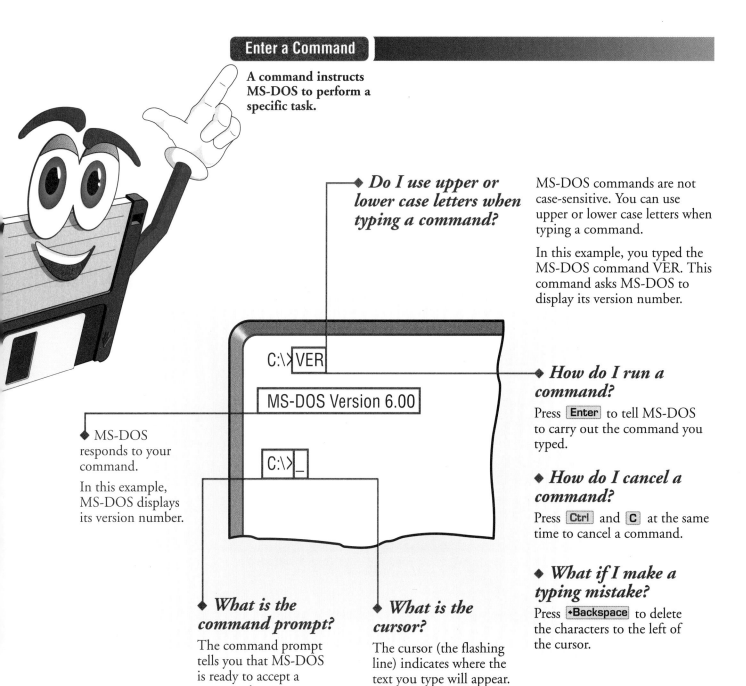

◆ **Do I use upper or lower case letters when typing a command?**

MS-DOS commands are not case-sensitive. You can use upper or lower case letters when typing a command.

In this example, you typed the MS-DOS command VER. This command asks MS-DOS to display its version number.

```
C:\>VER

MS-DOS Version 6.00

C:\>_
```

◆ MS-DOS responds to your command.

In this example, MS-DOS displays its version number.

◆ **How do I run a command?**

Press **Enter** to tell MS-DOS to carry out the command you typed.

◆ **How do I cancel a command?**

Press **Ctrl** and **C** at the same time to cancel a command.

◆ **What if I make a typing mistake?**

Press **◆Backspace** to delete the characters to the left of the cursor.

◆ **What is the command prompt?**

The command prompt tells you that MS-DOS is ready to accept a command.

◆ **What is the cursor?**

The cursor (the flashing line) indicates where the text you type will appear.

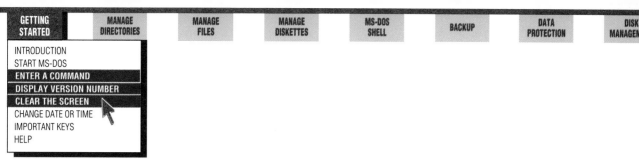

GETTING STARTED | MANAGE DIRECTORIES | MANAGE FILES | MANAGE DISKETTES | MS-DOS SHELL | BACKUP | DATA PROTECTION | DISK MANAGEMENT

INTRODUCTION
START MS-DOS
ENTER A COMMAND
DISPLAY VERSION NUMBER
CLEAR THE SCREEN
CHANGE DATE OR TIME
IMPORTANT KEYS
HELP

Display the MS-DOS Version Number

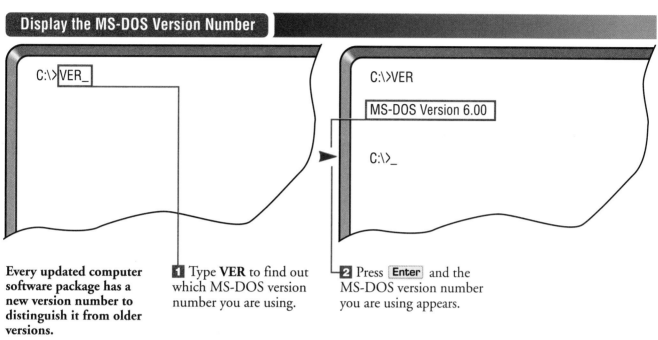

Every updated computer software package has a new version number to distinguish it from older versions.

1 Type **VER** to find out which MS-DOS version number you are using.

2 Press **Enter** and the MS-DOS version number you are using appears.

Clear the Screen

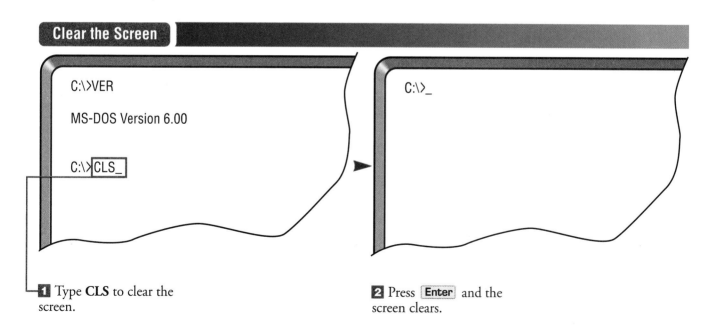

1 Type **CLS** to clear the screen.

2 Press **Enter** and the screen clears.

CHANGE DATE
OR TIME

Change the Date

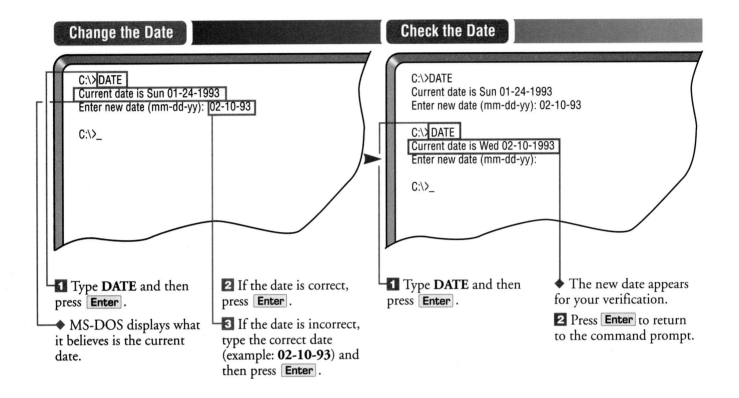

```
C:\>DATE
Current date is Sun 01-24-1993
Enter new date (mm-dd-yy): 02-10-93

C:\>_
```

Check the Date

```
C:\>DATE
Current date is Sun 01-24-1993
Enter new date (mm-dd-yy): 02-10-93

C:\>DATE
Current date is Wed 02-10-1993
Enter new date (mm-dd-yy):

C:\>_
```

1 Type **DATE** and then press **Enter**.

◆ MS-DOS displays what it believes is the current date.

2 If the date is correct, press **Enter**.

3 If the date is incorrect, type the correct date (example: **02-10-93**) and then press **Enter**.

1 Type **DATE** and then press **Enter**.

◆ The new date appears for your verification.

2 Press **Enter** to return to the command prompt.

◆ Most computers contain a battery that maintains the current date and time even when you turn your computer off.

However, sometimes you may need to change these settings (example: to adjust to daylight saving time).

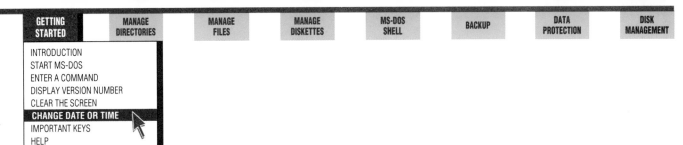

INTRODUCTION
START MS-DOS
ENTER A COMMAND
DISPLAY VERSION NUMBER
CLEAR THE SCREEN
CHANGE DATE OR TIME
IMPORTANT KEYS
HELP

Change the Time

Check the Time

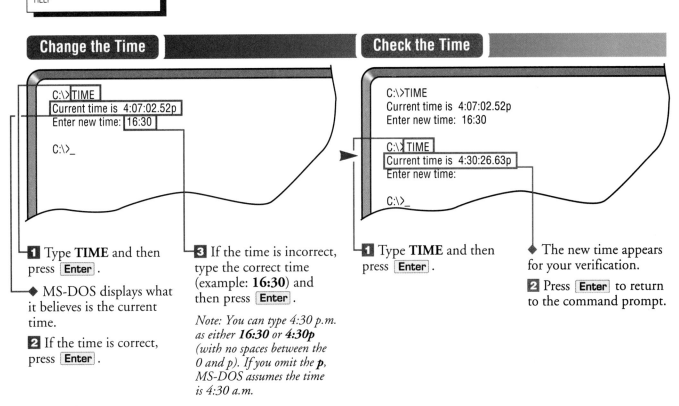

```
C:\>TIME
Current time is  4:07:02.52p
Enter new time:  16:30

C:\>_
```

```
C:\>TIME
Current time is  4:07:02.52p
Enter new time:  16:30

C:\>TIME
Current time is  4:30:26.63p
Enter new time:

C:\>_
```

1 Type **TIME** and then press **Enter**.

◆ MS-DOS displays what it believes is the current time.

2 If the time is correct, press **Enter**.

3 If the time is incorrect, type the correct time (example: **16:30**) and then press **Enter**.

*Note: You can type 4:30 p.m. as either **16:30** or **4:30p** (with no spaces between the 0 and p). If you omit the **p**, MS-DOS assumes the time is 4:30 a.m.*

1 Type **TIME** and then press **Enter**.

◆ The new time appears for your verification.

2 Press **Enter** to return to the command prompt.

RESTART MS-DOS

You may need to restart your computer if it is not responding properly or if the keyboard locks.

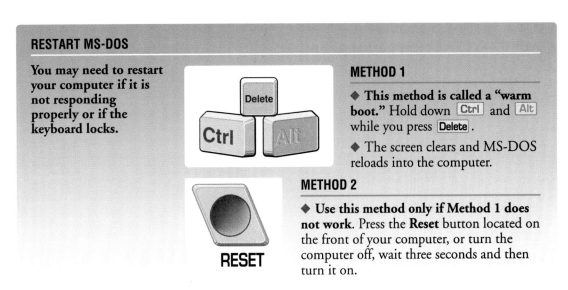

METHOD 1

◆ **This method is called a "warm boot."** Hold down **Ctrl** and **Alt** while you press **Delete**.

◆ The screen clears and MS-DOS reloads into the computer.

METHOD 2

◆ **Use this method only if Method 1 does not work.** Press the **Reset** button located on the front of your computer, or turn the computer off, wait three seconds and then turn it on.

IMPORTANT KEYS

The computer remembers the last MS-DOS command you typed. You can recall or modify the command using the F1, F2 or F3 function keys.

◆ F1 KEY

Press the F1 key to display the last command you typed, one character at a time.

◆ F2 KEY

Press the F2 key to display the last command you typed, up to a specified character. For example, if the last command you typed was ABCDEFGH and you press F2 and then E, the screen will display ABCD.

◆ F3 KEY

Press the F3 key to display the last command you typed.

◆ ESCAPE KEY

Press the Esc key to cancel a line of text you typed.

◆ CAPITALS LOCK

Press the Caps Lock key to switch the keys between upper (ABCD) and lower case (abcd) letters.

◆ SHIFT KEY

If you press the Shift key in combination with another key, you can change the case of a letter (example: a to A) or type a special character (example: $).

◆ ALTERNATE KEY

The Alt key works in combination with other keys to select MS-DOS Shell commands.

◆ SPACEBAR

Press the Spacebar to insert a blank space.

10

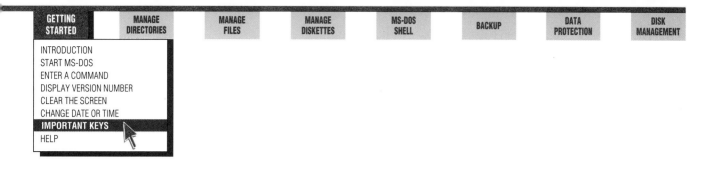

GETTING STARTED	MANAGE DIRECTORIES	MANAGE FILES	MANAGE DISKETTES	MS-DOS SHELL	BACKUP	DATA PROTECTION	DISK MANAGEMENT

INTRODUCTION
START MS-DOS
ENTER A COMMAND
DISPLAY VERSION NUMBER
CLEAR THE SCREEN
CHANGE DATE OR TIME
IMPORTANT KEYS
HELP

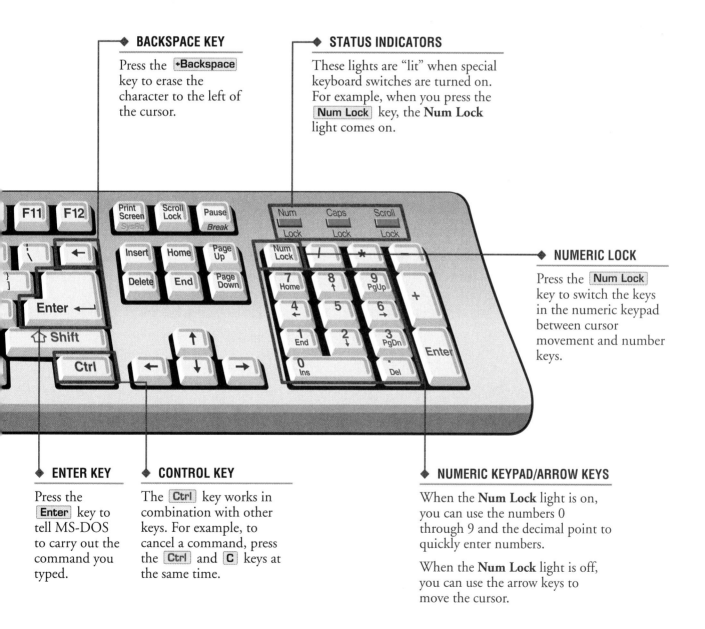

◆ BACKSPACE KEY

Press the `+Backspace` key to erase the character to the left of the cursor.

◆ STATUS INDICATORS

These lights are "lit" when special keyboard switches are turned on. For example, when you press the `Num Lock` key, the **Num Lock** light comes on.

◆ NUMERIC LOCK

Press the `Num Lock` key to switch the keys in the numeric keypad between cursor movement and number keys.

◆ ENTER KEY

Press the `Enter` key to tell MS-DOS to carry out the command you typed.

◆ CONTROL KEY

The `Ctrl` key works in combination with other keys. For example, to cancel a command, press the `Ctrl` and `C` keys at the same time.

◆ NUMERIC KEYPAD/ARROW KEYS

When the **Num Lock** light is on, you can use the numbers 0 through 9 and the decimal point to quickly enter numbers.

When the **Num Lock** light is off, you can use the arrow keys to move the cursor.

HELP

MS-DOS Help provides a complete glossary of MS-DOS commands. If you cannot remember how to perform a task, look up the command for an explanation.

General Help

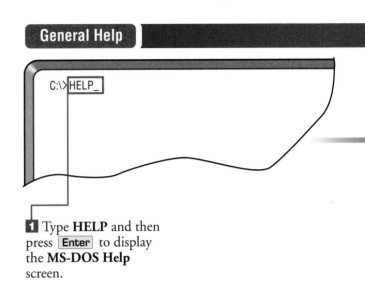

C:\>HELP_

1 Type **HELP** and then press **Enter** to display the **MS-DOS Help** screen.

Specific Help

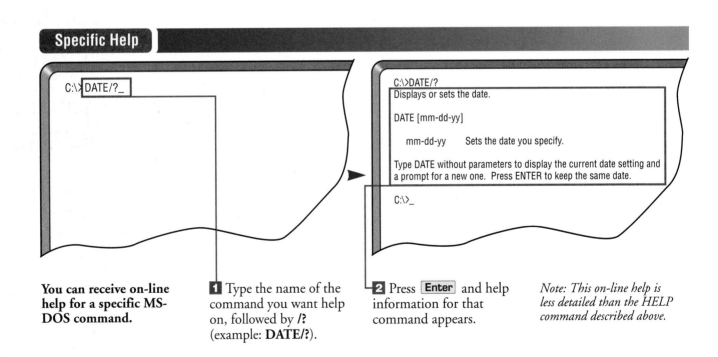

C:\>DATE/?_

```
C:\>DATE/?
Displays or sets the date.

DATE [mm-dd-yy]

    mm-dd-yy    Sets the date you specify.

Type DATE without parameters to display the current date setting and
a prompt for a new one.  Press ENTER to keep the same date.

C:\>_
```

You can receive on-line help for a specific MS-DOS command.

1 Type the name of the command you want help on, followed by **/?** (example: **DATE/?**).

2 Press **Enter** and help information for that command appears.

Note: This on-line help is less detailed than the HELP command described above.

| GETTING STARTED | MANAGE DIRECTORIES | MANAGE FILES | MANAGE DISKETTES | MS-DOS SHELL | BACKUP | DATA PROTECTION | DISK MANAGEMENT |

INTRODUCTION
START MS-DOS
ENTER A COMMAND
DISPLAY VERSION NUMBER
CLEAR THE SCREEN
CHANGE DATE OR TIME
IMPORTANT KEYS
HELP

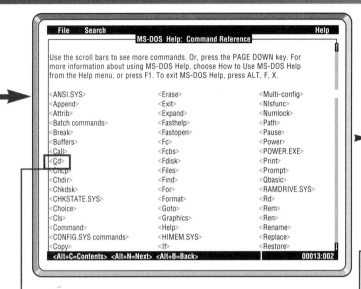

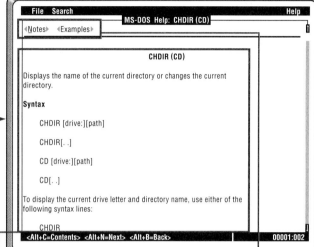

2 Use the ↓ , ↑ and **Tab** keys to position the cursor on the command you want help on (example: **Cd**).

Note: The cursor is the flashing line (_).

3 Press **Enter** and help information for that command appears.

4 To exit MS-DOS Help and return to the command prompt, press **Alt**, **F**, **X** .

▼ **Notes** displays additional information on the command.

▼ **Examples** displays ways to use the command.

To display either screen, press **Tab** until the cursor is on the heading and then press **Enter** .

TIP You can skip the Command Reference screen and go directly to the help screen that describes a particular command:

1 At the command prompt, type **HELP**.

2 Press the **Spacebar** and then type the command name (example: **Cd**).

3 Press **Enter** .

INTRODUCTION TO DRIVES

What are Drives?

◆ Your computer stores your programs and data in devices called "drives." A drive is similar to a filing cabinet because it stores information in an organized way.

◆ Most computers have one hard drive and one or two floppy drives. The hard drive is usually called drive C. The floppy drives are called drives A and B.

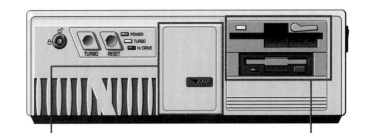

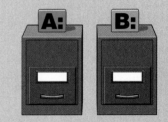

Hard drive (C:)

◆ A hard drive stores your programs and data. Most computers have at least one hard drive. This drive is called drive **C**.

Note: Some computers may have additional drives, depending on their setup.

Floppy drives (A: and B:)

◆ Floppy drives store your programs and data on removable media called diskettes (or floppy disks). Diskettes operate slower and store less data than hard drives.

If a computer has only one floppy drive, it is called drive **A**.

If a computer has two floppy drives, the second drive is called drive **B**.

TIP

DRIVE NAME

C: ─◆ A drive name consists of two parts: the letter and a colon (:). The colon represents the word "drive." For example, typing **C:** refers to the **C drive**.

GETTING STARTED	MANAGE DIRECTORIES	MANAGE FILES	MANAGE DISKETTES	MS-DOS SHELL	BACKUP	DATA PROTECTION	DISK MANAGEMENT

INTRODUCTION TO DRIVES
INTRODUCTION TO DIRECTORIES
MAKE A DIRECTORY
CHANGE DIRECTORIES
DISPLAY DIRECTORY TREE
REMOVE A DIRECTORY

What is the Current Drive?

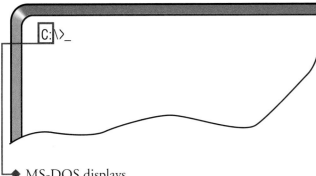

`C:\>_`

◆ MS-DOS displays the current drive on the computer screen. In this example, the current drive is **C:**.

When entering a command, type the drive name (example: C:). This tells MS-DOS which drive you want to work with. If you leave out the drive name, MS-DOS assumes you want the command to work with the current drive.

To simplify the typing of MS-DOS commands:

Make sure the current drive is:

C:	**A:**	**B:**
When you want a command to work with the **C drive**.	When you want a command to work with the **A drive**.	When you want a command to work with the **B drive**.

Change Drives

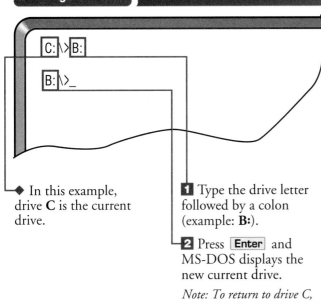

`C:\>B:`

`B:\>_`

◆ In this example, drive **C** is the current drive.

1 Type the drive letter followed by a colon (example: **B:**).

2 Press **Enter** and MS-DOS displays the new current drive.

Note: To return to drive C, type C: and then press **Enter** .

Before changing to a floppy drive, make sure you insert a diskette into the drive.

Note: For more information on floppy drives and diskettes, refer to page 50.

INTRODUCTION TO DIRECTORIES

What are Directories?

Directories are similar to the drawers and folders in a filing cabinet. They help you organize the programs and data stored on your computer.

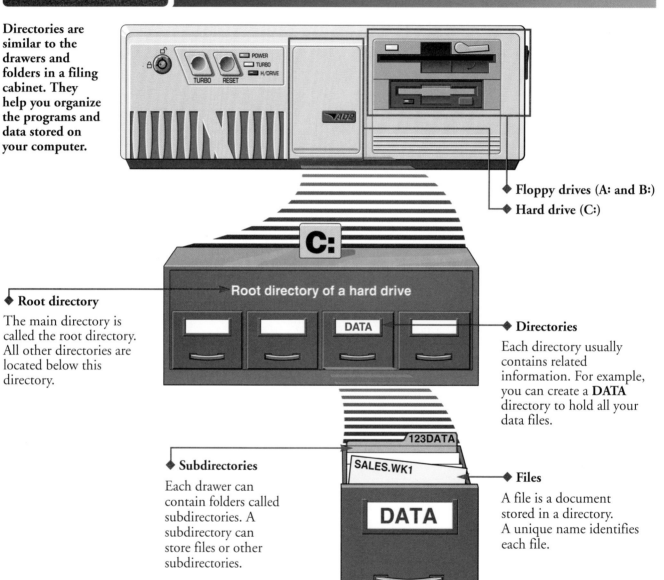

◆ **Floppy drives (A: and B:)**
◆ **Hard drive (C:)**

Root directory of a hard drive

◆ **Root directory**

The main directory is called the root directory. All other directories are located below this directory.

◆ **Directories**

Each directory usually contains related information. For example, you can create a **DATA** directory to hold all your data files.

◆ **Subdirectories**

Each drawer can contain folders called subdirectories. A subdirectory can store files or other subdirectories.

◆ **Files**

A file is a document stored in a directory. A unique name identifies each file.

GETTING STARTED	MANAGE DIRECTORIES	MANAGE FILES	MANAGE DISKETTES	MS-DOS SHELL	BACKUP	DATA PROTECTION	DISK MANAGEMENT

INTRODUCTION TO DRIVES
INTRODUCTION TO DIRECTORIES
MAKE A DIRECTORY
CHANGE DIRECTORIES
DISPLAY DIRECTORY TREE
REMOVE A DIRECTORY

What is a Path?

If you require a certain file, you must tell MS-DOS exactly how to find it. A "path" is the direction you tell MS-DOS to follow to locate that file.

For example, to find the SALES.WK1 file, you must:

Go to *the drawer labeled* **DATA**

Go to *the folder labeled* **123DATA**

Go to *the file labeled* **SALES.WK1**

Go to equals \

To instruct MS-DOS to retrieve the same file stored on your hard drive, replace the words Go to with \.

To retrieve this file, you must type:
\DATA\123DATA\SALES.WK1

MAKE A DIRECTORY

Make a Directory

The Make Directory command (typed as MD) lets you create a new directory.

Directories help you organize the programs and data stored on your hard and floppy drives.

The Make Directory command is:

MD	DRIVE	PATH	DIRECTORY NAME

MD	Stands for Make Directory.
DRIVE	Tells MS-DOS the drive where you want to create the new directory.
PATH	Tells MS-DOS the path to the new directory.
DIRECTORY NAME	Tells MS-DOS the name of the new directory.

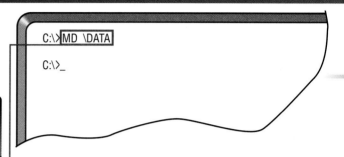

```
C:\>MD \DATA

C:\>_
```

Make the DATA directory

1 Type **MD** (for Make Directory) and then press the **Spacebar**.

2 Type the name of the new directory (example: **\DATA**).

3 Press **Enter** and the command prompt **C:\>** appears, indicating that MS-DOS created the directory.

TIP ◆ If you omit the drive and path, directories are created in the current drive and within the current directory.

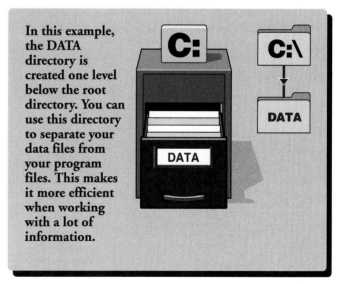

In this example, the DATA directory is created one level below the root directory. You can use this directory to separate your data files from your program files. This makes it more efficient when working with a lot of information.

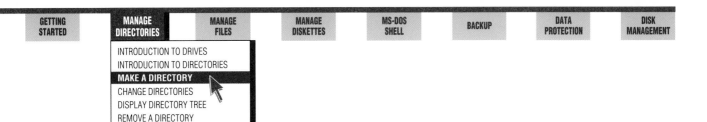

| GETTING STARTED | MANAGE DIRECTORIES | MANAGE FILES | MANAGE DISKETTES | MS-DOS SHELL | BACKUP | DATA PROTECTION | DISK MANAGEMENT |

INTRODUCTION TO DRIVES
INTRODUCTION TO DIRECTORIES
MAKE A DIRECTORY
CHANGE DIRECTORIES
DISPLAY DIRECTORY TREE
REMOVE A DIRECTORY

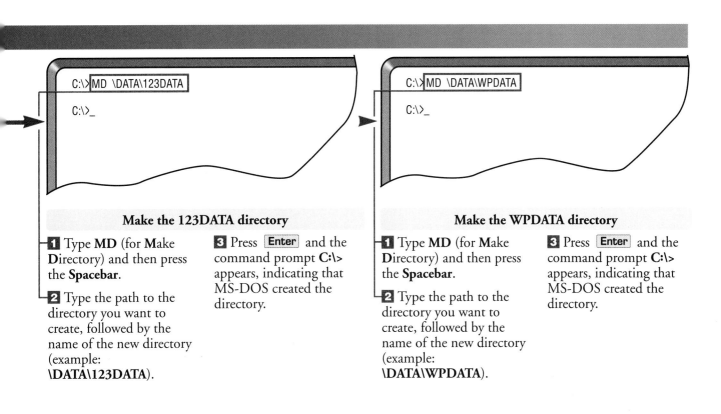

```
C:\> MD \DATA\123DATA

C:\>_
```

```
C:\> MD \DATA\WPDATA

C:\>_
```

Make the 123DATA directory

1 Type **MD** (for **M**ake **D**irectory) and then press the **Spacebar**.

2 Type the path to the directory you want to create, followed by the name of the new directory (example: **\DATA\123DATA**).

3 Press **Enter** and the command prompt **C:\>** appears, indicating that MS-DOS created the directory.

Make the WPDATA directory

1 Type **MD** (for **M**ake **D**irectory) and then press the **Spacebar**.

2 Type the path to the directory you want to create, followed by the name of the new directory (example: **\DATA\WPDATA**).

3 Press **Enter** and the command prompt **C:\>** appears, indicating that MS-DOS created the directory.

In this example, the 123DATA directory is created one level below the DATA directory. You can store all your spreadsheet files in this directory.

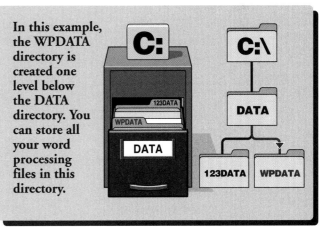

In this example, the WPDATA directory is created one level below the DATA directory. You can store all your word processing files in this directory.

CHANGE DIRECTORIES

The Change Directory command (typed as CD) allows you to navigate through your directory structure.

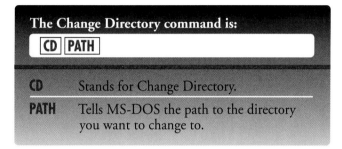

The Change Directory command is:

`CD` `PATH`

CD   Stands for Change Directory.

PATH   Tells MS-DOS the path to the directory you want to change to.

Change the Current Directory

In this example, the current directory is changed from the root directory to the 123DATA directory.

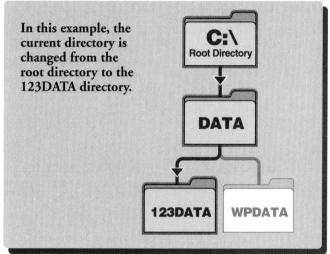

Move Up One Directory Level (Shortcut)

In this example, the current directory is changed from the 123DATA directory to the DATA directory.

This is a fast method of moving up the directory structure one level at a time.

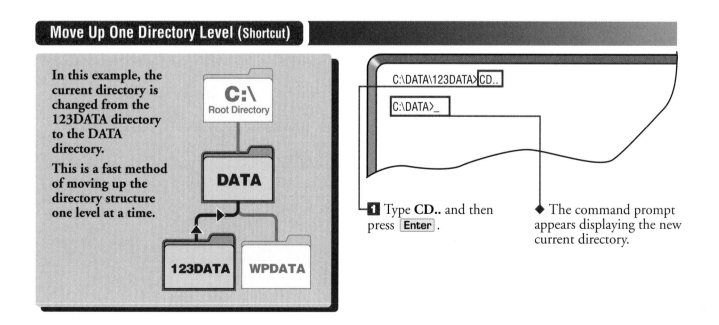

1 Type **CD..** and then press **Enter**.

◆ The command prompt appears displaying the new current directory.

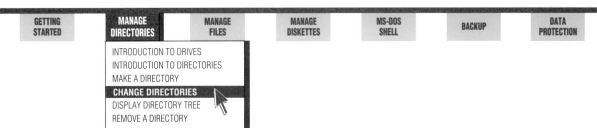

| GETTING STARTED | MANAGE DIRECTORIES | MANAGE FILES | MANAGE DISKETTES | MS-DOS SHELL | BACKUP | DATA PROTECTION | DISK MANAGEMENT |

INTRODUCTION TO DRIVES
INTRODUCTION TO DIRECTORIES
MAKE A DIRECTORY
CHANGE DIRECTORIES
DISPLAY DIRECTORY TREE
REMOVE A DIRECTORY

```
C:\>CD \DATA\123DATA

C:\DATA\123DATA>_
```

1 Type **CD** (for **C**hange **D**irectory) and then press the **Spacebar**.

2 Type the path to the directory you want to change to (example: **\DATA\123DATA**).

3 Press `Enter` and the command prompt appears displaying the new current directory.

Move Down One Directory Level (Shortcut)

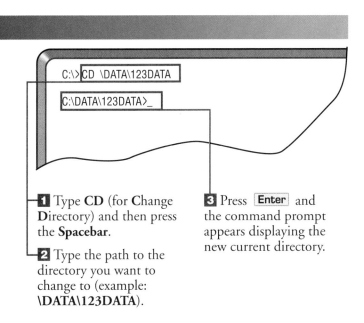

In this example, the current directory is changed from the DATA directory to the WPDATA directory.

This is a fast method of moving down the directory structure one level at a time.

```
C:\DATA>CD WPDATA

C:\DATA\WPDATA>_
```

1 Type **CD** (for **C**hange **D**irectory) and then press the **Spacebar**.

2 Type the name of the directory you want to change to (example: **WPDATA**).

3 Press `Enter` and the command prompt appears displaying the new current directory.

*Note: To change from any directory to the root directory, type **CD** and then press* `Enter`.

DISPLAY DIRECTORY TREE

The Tree command visually displays the structure of a directory's contents. This command is extremely helpful if you cannot remember how your directories are organized.

The Tree command is:

TREE | **DRIVE** | **PATH** | **/F**

DRIVE	Tells MS-DOS the drive that contains the directory structure you want to display.
PATH	Tells MS-DOS where to start displaying the directory structure.
/F	Tells MS-DOS to list all files in the displayed directories.

Note: If you omit the drive and path, MS-DOS displays a directory structure of the current drive, starting from the current directory.

Display Only Directories

In this example, all directories starting from the root directory (C:\) are displayed.

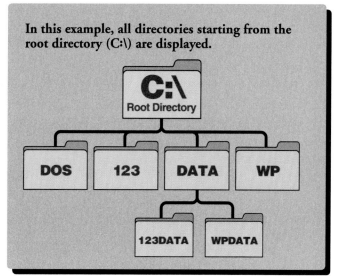

PRINT A DIRECTORY STRUCTURE

◆ Type **>PRN** after the **TREE** command to direct the output to your printer instead of the screen.

For example, to print the directory structure of the DOS directory, including all files, type:

TREE \DOS/F>PRN

Note: Refer to your printer manual to determine if your printer supports the extended character set. If it does not, type /A after the Tree command (example: TREE \DOS/F/A>PRN). This adds vertical bars, hyphens, etc. to help your printer draw the directory structure.

Display Files and Directories

In this example, all subdirectories and files starting from the DOS directory are displayed.

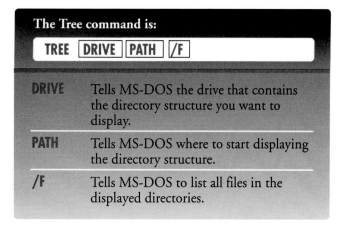

INTRODUCTION TO DRIVES
INTRODUCTION TO DIRECTORIES
MAKE A DIRECTORY
CHANGE DIRECTORIES
DISPLAY DIRECTORY TREE
REMOVE A DIRECTORY

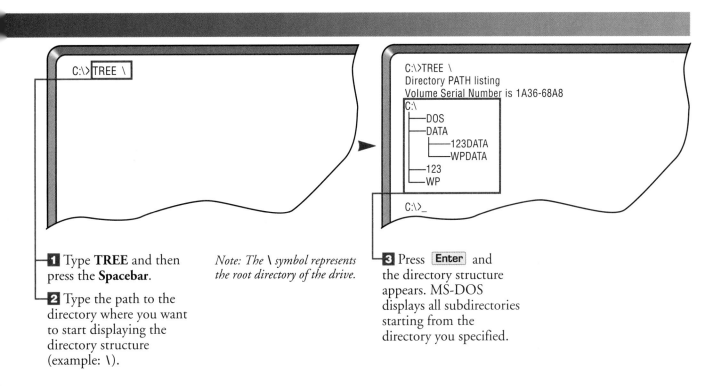

```
C:\>TREE \
```

```
C:\>TREE \
Directory PATH listing
Volume Serial Number is 1A36-68A8
C:\
├──DOS
├──DATA
│     ├──────123DATA
│     └──────WPDATA
├──123
└──WP

C:\>_
```

1 Type **TREE** and then press the **Spacebar**.

2 Type the path to the directory where you want to start displaying the directory structure (example: \).

Note: The \ symbol represents the root directory of the drive.

3 Press **Enter** and the directory structure appears. MS-DOS displays all subdirectories starting from the directory you specified.

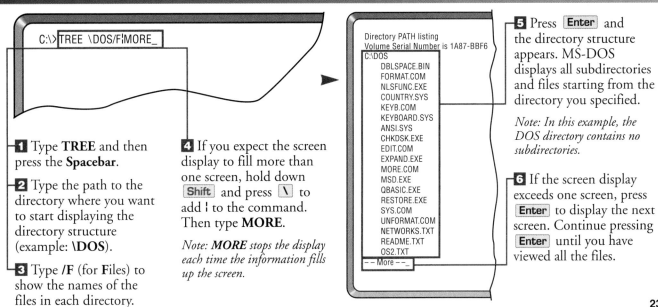

```
C:\>TREE \DOS/F¦MORE_
```

```
Directory PATH listing
Volume Serial Number is 1A87-BBF6
C:\DOS
     DBLSPACE.BIN
     FORMAT.COM
     NLSFUNC.EXE
     COUNTRY.SYS
     KEYB.COM
     KEYBOARD.SYS
     ANSI.SYS
     CHKDSK.EXE
     EDIT.COM
     EXPAND.EXE
     MORE.COM
     MSD.EXE
     QBASIC.EXE
     RESTORE.EXE
     SYS.COM
     UNFORMAT.COM
     NETWORKS.TXT
     README.TXT
     OS2.TXT
- - More - -_
```

1 Type **TREE** and then press the **Spacebar**.

2 Type the path to the directory where you want to start displaying the directory structure (example: **\DOS**).

3 Type **/F** (for Files) to show the names of the files in each directory.

4 If you expect the screen display to fill more than one screen, hold down **Shift** and press **** to add ¦ to the command. Then type **MORE**.

Note: MORE stops the display each time the information fills up the screen.

5 Press **Enter** and the directory structure appears. MS-DOS displays all subdirectories and files starting from the directory you specified.

Note: In this example, the DOS directory contains no subdirectories.

6 If the screen display exceeds one screen, press **Enter** to display the next screen. Continue pressing **Enter** until you have viewed all the files.

REMOVE A DIRECTORY

Remove a Directory

The **Remove Directory** command (typed as RD) allows you to remove empty directories from your drive.

> **The Remove Directory command is:**
>
> `RD` `DRIVE` `PATH`
>
> | | |
> |---|---|
> | **RD** | Stands for Remove Directory. |
> | **DRIVE** | Tells MS-DOS the drive that contains the directory you want to remove. |
> | **PATH** | Tells MS-DOS the path to the directory you want to remove. |

In this example, the 123DATA directory is removed.

TIP

◆ If you omit the drive, MS-DOS assumes the current drive contains the directory you want to remove.

INTRODUCTION TO DRIVES
INTRODUCTION TO DIRECTORIES
MAKE A DIRECTORY
CHANGE DIRECTORIES
DISPLAY DIRECTORY TREE
REMOVE A DIRECTORY

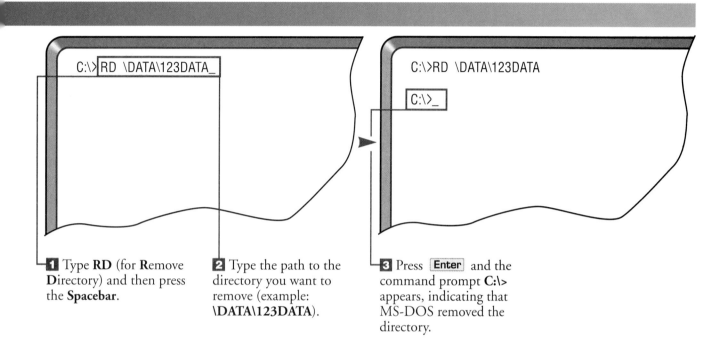

C:\>RD \DATA\123DATA_

C:\>RD \DATA\123DATA

C:\>_

1 Type **RD** (for **R**emove **D**irectory) and then press the **Spacebar**.

2 Type the path to the directory you want to remove (example: **\DATA\123DATA**).

3 Press **Enter** and the command prompt **C:\>** appears, indicating that MS-DOS removed the directory.

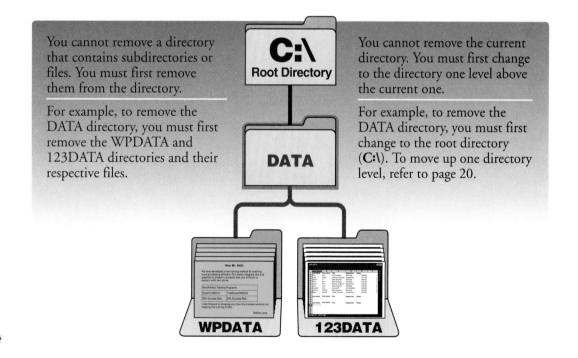

You cannot remove a directory that contains subdirectories or files. You must first remove them from the directory.

For example, to remove the DATA directory, you must first remove the WPDATA and 123DATA directories and their respective files.

You cannot remove the current directory. You must first change to the directory one level above the current one.

For example, to remove the DATA directory, you must first change to the root directory (**C:**). To move up one directory level, refer to page 20.

C:
Root Directory

DATA

WPDATA

123DATA

INTRODUCTION TO FILES

What is a File?

A file is a named collection of information stored on a disk.

PROGRAM FILES

Program files enable you to write letters, analyze numbers, sort data, draw pictures and even play games.

DATA FILES

Data files are documents you create using program files.

File Location

If you require a certain file, you must tell MS-DOS exactly how to find it. A "path" is the direction you tell MS-DOS to follow to locate that file.

IN EVERYDAY LANGUAGE...

To find the **PROJECT3.WK1** file, you must:

Go to the drawer labeled **DATA**, then

Go to the folder labeled **123DATA**, then

Go to the file labeled **PROJECT3.WK1**

Go to equals \

IN COMPUTER LANGUAGE...

To retrieve the **PROJECT3.WK1** file, you must type:

\DATA\123DATA\PROJECT3.WK1

| GETTING STARTED | MANAGE DIRECTORIES | MANAGE FILES | | MANAGE DISKETTES | | MS-DOS SHELL | BACKUP | DATA PROTECTION | DISK MANAGEMENT |

INTRODUCTION TO FILES
INTRODUCTION TO WILDCARDS
DIRECTORY CONTENTS
SORT FILES
SEARCH FOR FILES

COPY FILES
MOVE FILES
RENAME FILES
DELETE FILES

File Names

A file name consists of two parts: the name and the extension. You must separate these parts with a period.

PROJECT3 . WK1

◆ **Period**
A period must separate the name and the extension.

◆ **Name**
The name describes the contents of a file. It can have up to 8 characters.

◆ **Extension**
The extension describes the type of information a file contains. It can have up to 3 characters.

FILE NAME RULES

The following characters are allowed:

◆ The letters A to Z, upper or lower case

◆ The numbers 0 through 9

◆ The symbols _ ^ $ ~ ! # % & - { } @ ` ( )

◆ The file name cannot contain a period, blank space or comma

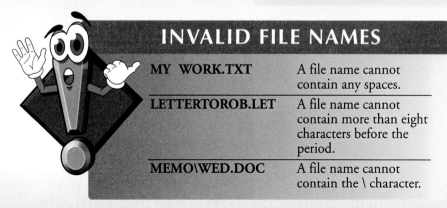

◆ Each file in a directory must have a unique name.

INVALID FILE NAMES

MY WORK.TXT	A file name cannot contain any spaces.
LETTERTOROB.LET	A file name cannot contain more than eight characters before the period.
MEMO\WED.DOC	A file name cannot contain the \ character.

COMMON EXTENSIONS

Program and data files normally have unique extensions to distinguish their files from others.

Word Processing Files
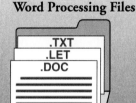
.TXT
.LET
.DOC

Spreadsheet Files

.WK3
.WK1
.XLS

Program Files

.BAT
.COM
.EXE

INTRODUCTION TO WILDCARDS

What are Wildcards?

You can use wildcards with certain commands to enable you to work with several files at the same time.

There are two wildcards: the asterisk (*) and the question mark (?).

Using the * Wildcard

The asterisk (*) represents one or more characters in a file name.

MEMO.* includes all files named MEMO, with any extension

*.LET includes all files with the LET extension

A*.* includes all files starting with the letter A, with any extension

. includes all files

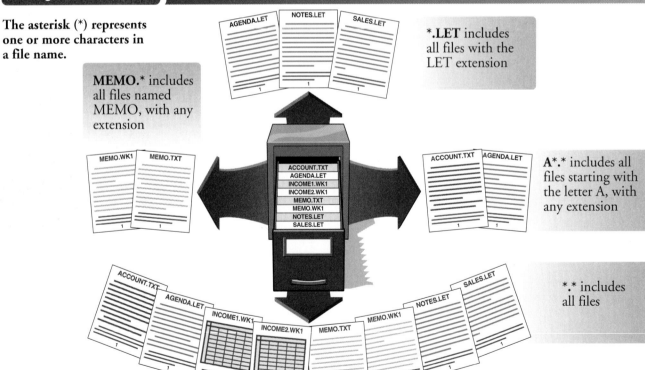

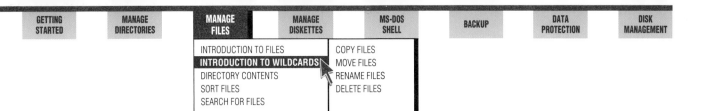

| GETTING STARTED | MANAGE DIRECTORIES | MANAGE FILES | MANAGE DISKETTES | MS-DOS SHELL | BACKUP | DATA PROTECTION | DISK MANAGEMENT |

INTRODUCTION TO FILES
INTRODUCTION TO WILDCARDS
DIRECTORY CONTENTS
SORT FILES
SEARCH FOR FILES

COPY FILES
MOVE FILES
RENAME FILES
DELETE FILES

Using the ? Wildcard

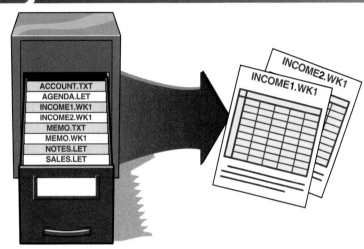

The question mark (?) represents a single character in a file name.

ACCOUNT.TXT
AGENDA.LET
INCOME1.WK1
INCOME2.WK1
MEMO.TXT
MEMO.WK1
NOTES.LET
SALES.LET

INCOME2.WK1
INCOME1.WK1

INCOME?.WK1 includes all files starting with INCOME, followed by any character and then .WK1

CREATING PRACTICE FILES

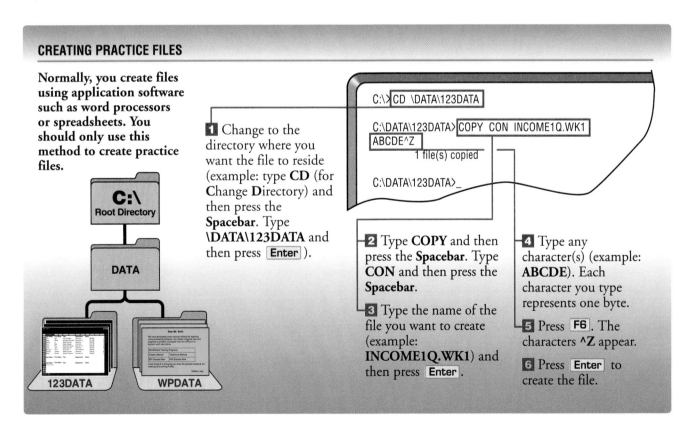

Normally, you create files using application software such as word processors or spreadsheets. You should only use this method to create practice files.

C:
Root Directory

DATA

123DATA   WPDATA

```
C:\> CD \DATA\123DATA

C:\DATA\123DATA> COPY CON INCOME1Q.WK1
ABCDE^Z
        1 file(s) copied

C:\DATA\123DATA>_
```

1 Change to the directory where you want the file to reside (example: type **CD** (for **C**hange **D**irectory) and then press the **Spacebar**. Type **\DATA\123DATA** and then press **Enter**).

2 Type **COPY** and then press the **Spacebar**. Type **CON** and then press the **Spacebar**.

3 Type the name of the file you want to create (example: **INCOME1Q.WK1**) and then press **Enter**.

4 Type any character(s) (example: **ABCDE**). Each character you type represents one byte.

5 Press **F6**. The characters **^Z** appear.

6 Press **Enter** to create the file.

DIRECTORY CONTENTS

The Directory command (typed as DIR) lists all the subdirectories and files within a directory. It also displays the size of the files and the date and time they were last modified.

Use this command if you cannot remember the contents of a particular directory.

The Directory command is:

DIR	DRIVE	PATH

DIR	Stands for DIRectory.
DRIVE	Tells MS-DOS the drive containing the directory whose contents you want to display.
PATH	Tells MS-DOS the path to the directory whose contents you want to display.

Note: If you omit the drive and path, MS-DOS displays the subdirectories and files of the current drive and directory.

TO DISPLAY ONLY DIRECTORIES

Type **/AD** after the **DIR** command.

For example, to display only the directories in the DOS directory, type: **DIR \DOS /AD**

TO DISPLAY ONLY FILES

Type **/A-D** after the **DIR** command.

For example, to display only the files in the DOS directory, type: **DIR \DOS /A-D**

TO PRINT THE CONTENTS OF A DIRECTORY

Type **>PRN** after the **DIR** command.

For example, to print the contents of the DOS directory, type: **DIR \DOS >PRN**

Display the Contents of a Directory

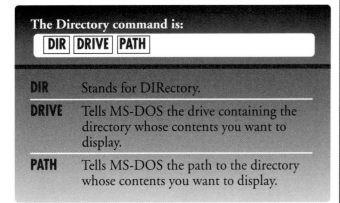

C:\> DIR \DATA\123DATA_

1 Type **DIR** (for **DIR**ectory) and then press the **Spacebar**.

2 Type the path to the directory whose contents you want to display (example: **\DATA\123DATA**).

3 Press **Enter** and the contents of the directory appear.

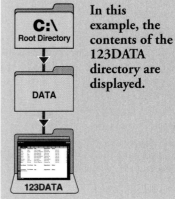

In this example, the contents of the 123DATA directory are displayed.

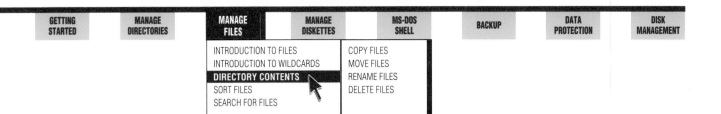

INTRODUCTION TO FILES
INTRODUCTION TO WILDCARDS
DIRECTORY CONTENTS
SORT FILES
SEARCH FOR FILES

COPY FILES
MOVE FILES
RENAME FILES
DELETE FILES

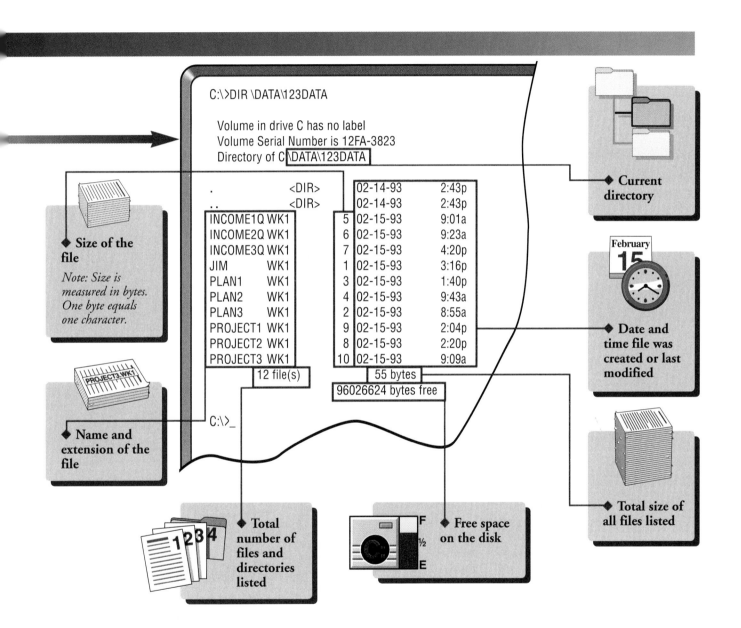

C:\>DIR \DATA\123DATA

Volume in drive C has no label
Volume Serial Number is 12FA-3823
Directory of C:\DATA\123DATA

.	<DIR>		02-14-93	2:43p
..	<DIR>		02-14-93	2:43p
INCOME1Q WK1		5	02-15-93	9:01a
INCOME2Q WK1		6	02-15-93	9:23a
INCOME3Q WK1		7	02-15-93	4:20p
JIM WK1		1	02-15-93	3:16p
PLAN1 WK1		3	02-15-93	1:40p
PLAN2 WK1		4	02-15-93	9:43a
PLAN3 WK1		2	02-15-93	8:55a
PROJECT1 WK1		9	02-15-93	2:04p
PROJECT2 WK1		8	02-15-93	2:20p
PROJECT3 WK1		10	02-15-93	9:09a
	12 file(s)		55 bytes	

96026624 bytes free

C:\>_

◆ **Current directory**

◆ **Size of the file**

Note: Size is measured in bytes. One byte equals one character.

◆ **Name and extension of the file**

February
15

◆ **Date and time file was created or last modified**

◆ **Total size of all files listed**

◆ **Total number of files and directories listed**

F
½
E

◆ **Free space on the disk**

DIRECTORY CONTENTS

If you cannot view the entire contents of a directory on one screen, MS-DOS offers two options.

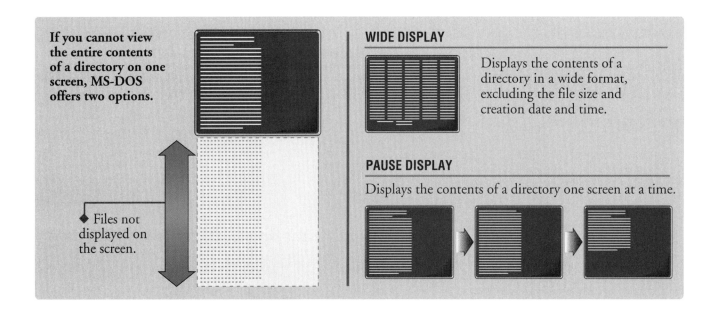

◆ Files not displayed on the screen.

WIDE DISPLAY

Displays the contents of a directory in a wide format, excluding the file size and creation date and time.

PAUSE DISPLAY

Displays the contents of a directory one screen at a time.

Wide Display

`C:\> DIR \DOS /W_`

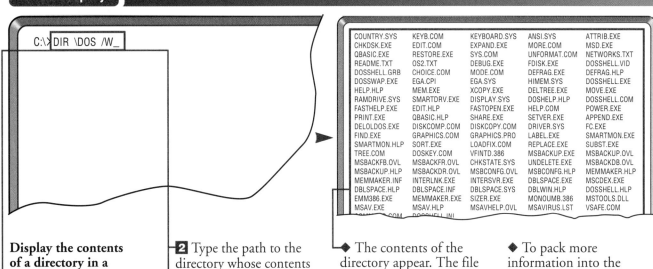

COUNTRY.SYS	KEYB.COM	KEYBOARD.SYS	ANSI.SYS	ATTRIB.EXE
CHKDSK.EXE	EDIT.COM	EXPAND.EXE	MORE.COM	MSD.EXE
QBASIC.EXE	RESTORE.EXE	SYS.COM	UNFORMAT.COM	NETWORKS.TXT
README.TXT	OS2.TXT	DEBUG.EXE	FDISK.EXE	DOSSHELL.VID
DOSSHELL.GRB	CHOICE.COM	MODE.COM	DEFRAG.EXE	DEFRAG.HLP
DOSSWAP.EXE	EGA.CPI	EGA.SYS	HIMEM.SYS	DOSSHELL.EXE
HELP.HLP	MEM.EXE	XCOPY.EXE	DELTREE.EXE	MOVE.EXE
RAMDRIVE.SYS	SMARTDRV.EXE	DISPLAY.SYS	DOSHELP.HLP	DOSSHELL.COM
FASTHELP.EXE	EDIT.HLP	FASTOPEN.EXE	HELP.COM	POWER.EXE
PRINT.EXE	QBASIC.HLP	SHARE.EXE	SETVER.EXE	APPEND.EXE
DELOLDOS.EXE	DISKCOMP.COM	DISKCOPY.COM	DRIVER.SYS	FC.EXE
FIND.EXE	GRAPHICS.COM	GRAPHICS.PRO	LABEL.EXE	SMARTMON.EXE
SMARTMON.HLP	SORT.EXE	LOADFIX.COM	REPLACE.EXE	SUBST.EXE
TREE.COM	DOSKEY.COM	VFINTD.386	MSBACKUP.EXE	MSBACKUP.OVL
MSBACKFB.OVL	MSBACKFR.OVL	CHKSTATE.SYS	UNDELETE.EXE	MSBACKDB.OVL
MSBACKUP.HLP	MSBACKDR.OVL	MSBCONFG.OVL	MSBCONFG.HLP	MEMMAKER.HLP
MEMMAKER.INF	INTERLNK.EXE	INTERSVR.EXE	DBLSPACE.EXE	MSCDEX.EXE
DBLSPACE.HLP	DBLSPACE.INF	DBLSPACE.SYS	DBLWIN.HLP	DOSSHELL.HLP
EMM386.EXE	MEMMAKER.EXE	SIZER.EXE	MONOUMB.386	MSTOOLS.DLL
MSAV.EXE	MSAV.HLP	MSAVHELP.OVL	MSAVIRUS.LST	VSAFE.COM

Display the contents of a directory in a wide format.

1 Type **DIR** (for **DIR**ectory) and then press the **Spacebar**.

2 Type the path to the directory whose contents you want to display (example: **\DOS**) and then press the **Spacebar**.

3 Type **/W** (for **W**ide) and then press **Enter**.

◆ The contents of the directory appear. The file names are listed in a wide format.

◆ To pack more information into the display, MS-DOS omits the file size and creation date and time.

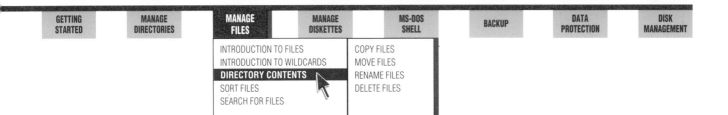

| GETTING STARTED | MANAGE DIRECTORIES | MANAGE FILES | MANAGE DISKETTES | MS-DOS SHELL | BACKUP | DATA PROTECTION | DISK MANAGEMENT |

INTRODUCTION TO FILES
INTRODUCTION TO WILDCARDS
DIRECTORY CONTENTS
SORT FILES
SEARCH FOR FILES

COPY FILES
MOVE FILES
RENAME FILES
DELETE FILES

Pause Display

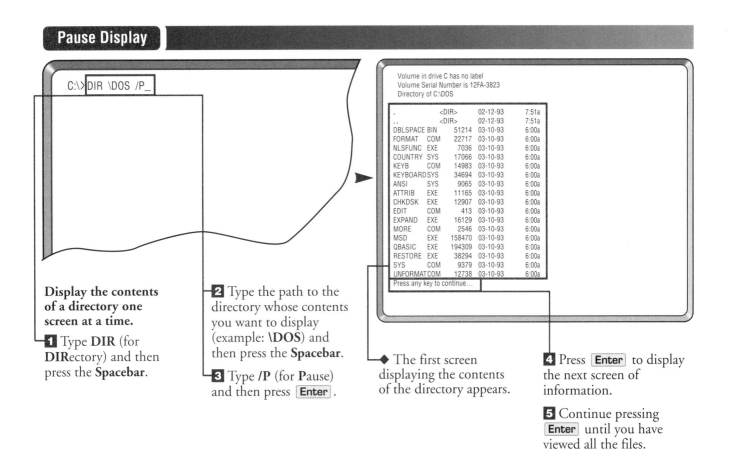

```
C:\> DIR \DOS /P_
```

```
Volume in drive C has no label
Volume Serial Number is 12FA-3823
Directory of C:\DOS

.                <DIR>        02-12-93    7:51a
..               <DIR>        02-12-93    7:51a
DBLSPACE BIN     51214        03-10-93    6:00a
FORMAT   COM     22717        03-10-93    6:00a
NLSFUNC  EXE      7036        03-10-93    6:00a
COUNTRY  SYS     17066        03-10-93    6:00a
KEYB     COM     14983        03-10-93    6:00a
KEYBOARD SYS     34694        03-10-93    6:00a
ANSI     SYS      9065        03-10-93    6:00a
ATTRIB   EXE     11165        03-10-93    6:00a
CHKDSK   EXE     12907        03-10-93    6:00a
EDIT     COM       413        03-10-93    6:00a
EXPAND   EXE     16129        03-10-93    6:00a
MORE     COM      2546        03-10-93    6:00a
MSD      EXE    158470        03-10-93    6:00a
QBASIC   EXE    194309        03-10-93    6:00a
RESTORE  EXE     38294        03-10-93    6:00a
SYS      COM      9379        03-10-93    6:00a
UNFORMAT COM     12738        03-10-93    6:00a
Press any key to continue...
```

Display the contents of a directory one screen at a time.

1 Type **DIR** (for **DIR**ectory) and then press the **Spacebar**.

2 Type the path to the directory whose contents you want to display (example: **\DOS**) and then press the **Spacebar**.

3 Type **/P** (for **P**ause) and then press **Enter**.

◆ The first screen displaying the contents of the directory appears.

4 Press **Enter** to display the next screen of information.

5 Continue pressing **Enter** until you have viewed all the files.

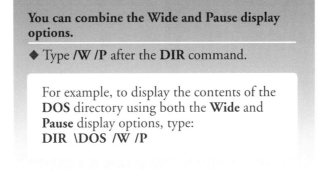

You can combine the Wide and Pause display options.

◆ Type **/W /P** after the **DIR** command.

For example, to display the contents of the **DOS** directory using both the **Wide** and **Pause** display options, type:
DIR \DOS /W /P

33

DIRECTORY CONTENTS

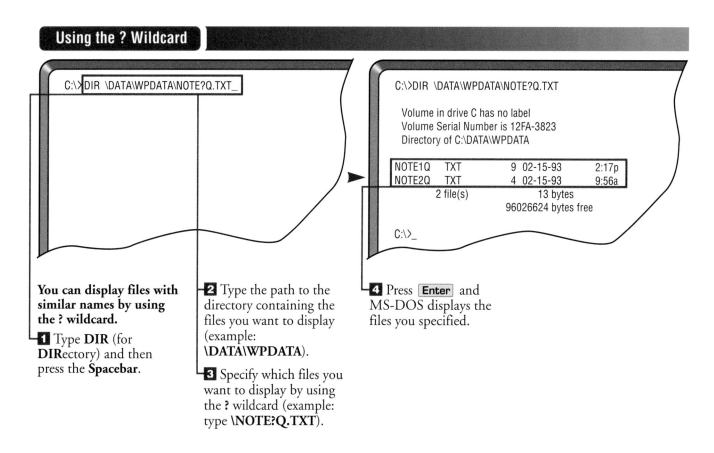

`C:\>DIR  \DATA\WPDATA\NOTE?Q.TXT_`

`C:\>DIR  \DATA\WPDATA\NOTE?Q.TXT`

Volume in drive C has no label
Volume Serial Number is 12FA-3823
Directory of C:\DATA\WPDATA

NOTE1Q	TXT	9	02-15-93	2:17p
NOTE2Q	TXT	4	02-15-93	9:56a
	2 file(s)		13 bytes	
			96026624 bytes free	

`C:\>_`

You can display files with similar names by using the ? wildcard.

1 Type **DIR** (for **DIR**ectory) and then press the **Spacebar**.

2 Type the path to the directory containing the files you want to display (example: **\DATA\WPDATA**).

3 Specify which files you want to display by using the **?** wildcard (example: type **\NOTE?Q.TXT**).

4 Press **Enter** and MS-DOS displays the files you specified.

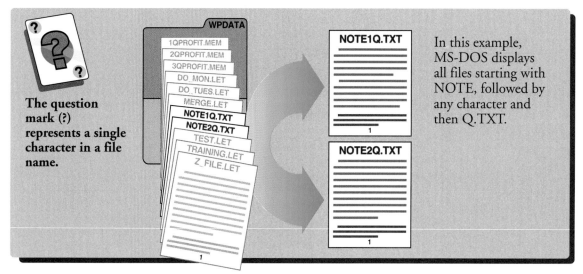

The question mark (?) represents a single character in a file name.

In this example, MS-DOS displays all files starting with NOTE, followed by any character and then Q.TXT.

34

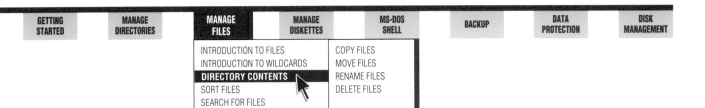

GETTING STARTED	MANAGE DIRECTORIES	MANAGE FILES	MANAGE DISKETTES	MS-DOS SHELL	BACKUP	DATA PROTECTION	DISK MANAGEMENT

INTRODUCTION TO FILES   COPY FILES
INTRODUCTION TO WILDCARDS MOVE FILES
DIRECTORY CONTENTS   RENAME FILES
SORT FILES   DELETE FILES
SEARCH FOR FILES

Using the * Wildcard

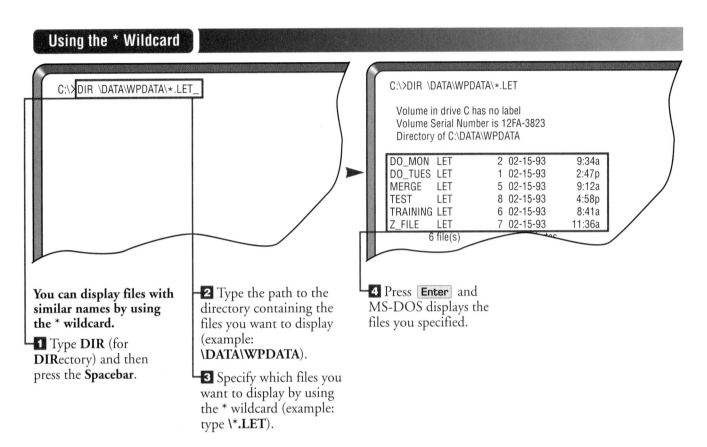

```
C:\>DIR \DATA\WPDATA\*.LET_
```

```
C:\>DIR \DATA\WPDATA\*.LET

   Volume in drive C has no label
   Volume Serial Number is 12FA-3823
   Directory of C:\DATA\WPDATA

DO_MON   LET      2 02-15-93     9:34a
DO_TUES  LET      1 02-15-93     2:47p
MERGE    LET      5 02-15-93     9:12a
TEST     LET      8 02-15-93     4:58p
TRAINING LET      6 02-15-93     8:41a
Z_FILE   LET      7 02-15-93    11:36a
        6 file(s)
```

You can display files with similar names by using the * wildcard.

1 Type **DIR** (for **DIR**ectory) and then press the **Spacebar**.

2 Type the path to the directory containing the files you want to display (example: **\DATA\WPDATA**).

3 Specify which files you want to display by using the * wildcard (example: type ***.LET**).

4 Press **Enter** and MS-DOS displays the files you specified.

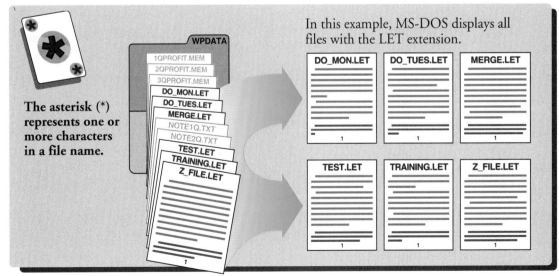

The asterisk (*) represents one or more characters in a file name.

In this example, MS-DOS displays all files with the LET extension.

WPDATA
1QPROFIT.MEM
2QPROFIT.MEM
3QPROFIT.MEM
DO_MON.LET
DO_TUES.LET
MERGE.LET
NOTE1Q.TXT
NOTE2Q.TXT
TEST.LET
TRAINING.LET
Z_FILE.LET

DO_MON.LET   DO_TUES.LET   MERGE.LET

TEST.LET   TRAINING.LET   Z_FILE.LET

SORT
FILES

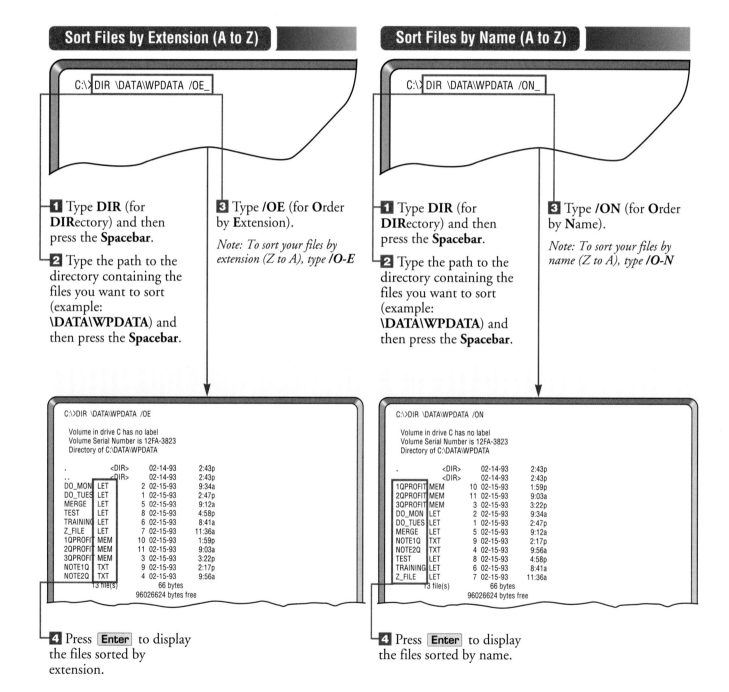

Sort Files by Extension (A to Z)

`C:\>DIR \DATA\WPDATA /OE_`

1 Type **DIR** (for **DIR**ectory) and then press the **Spacebar**.

2 Type the path to the directory containing the files you want to sort (example: **\DATA\WPDATA**) and then press the **Spacebar**.

3 Type **/OE** (for **O**rder by **E**xtension).

*Note: To sort your files by extension (Z to A), type **/O-E***

```
C:\>DIR \DATA\WPDATA /OE

    Volume in drive C has no label
    Volume Serial Number is 12FA-3823
    Directory of C:\DATA\WPDATA

.            <DIR>       02-14-93    2:43p
..           <DIR>       02-14-93    2:43p
DO_MON   LET         2   02-15-93    9:34a
DO_TUES  LET         1   02-15-93    2:47p
MERGE    LET         5   02-15-93    9:12a
TEST     LET         8   02-15-93    4:58p
TRAINING LET         6   02-15-93    8:41a
Z_FILE   LET         7   02-15-93   11:36a
1QPROFIT MEM        10   02-15-93    1:59p
2QPROFIT MEM        11   02-15-93    9:03a
3QPROFIT MEM         3   02-15-93    3:22p
NOTE1Q   TXT         9   02-15-93    2:17p
NOTE2Q   TXT         4   02-15-93    9:56a
       13 file(s)          66 bytes
                   96026624 bytes free
```

4 Press **Enter** to display the files sorted by extension.

Sort Files by Name (A to Z)

`C:\> DIR \DATA\WPDATA /ON_`

1 Type **DIR** (for **DIR**ectory) and then press the **Spacebar**.

2 Type the path to the directory containing the files you want to sort (example: **\DATA\WPDATA**) and then press the **Spacebar**.

3 Type **/ON** (for **O**rder by **N**ame).

*Note: To sort your files by name (Z to A), type **/O-N***

```
C:\>DIR \DATA\WPDATA /ON

    Volume in drive C has no label
    Volume Serial Number is 12FA-3823
    Directory of C:\DATA\WPDATA

.            <DIR>       02-14-93    2:43p
..           <DIR>       02-14-93    2:43p
1QPROFIT MEM        10   02-15-93    1:59p
2QPROFIT MEM        11   02-15-93    9:03a
3QPROFIT MEM         3   02-15-93    3:22p
DO_MON   LET         2   02-15-93    9:34a
DO_TUES  LET         1   02-15-93    2:47p
MERGE    LET         5   02-15-93    9:12a
NOTE1Q   TXT         9   02-15-93    2:17p
NOTE2Q   TXT         4   02-15-93    9:56a
TEST     LET         8   02-15-93    4:58p
TRAINING LET         6   02-15-93    8:41a
Z_FILE   LET         7   02-15-93   11:36a
       13 file(s)          66 bytes
                   96026624 bytes free
```

4 Press **Enter** to display the files sorted by name.

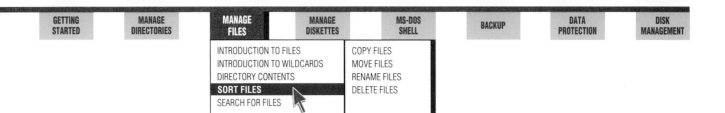

| GETTING STARTED | MANAGE DIRECTORIES | MANAGE FILES | MANAGE DISKETTES | MS-DOS SHELL | BACKUP | DATA PROTECTION | DISK MANAGEMENT |

INTRODUCTION TO FILES   COPY FILES
INTRODUCTION TO WILDCARDS   MOVE FILES
DIRECTORY CONTENTS   RENAME FILES
SORT FILES   DELETE FILES
SEARCH FOR FILES

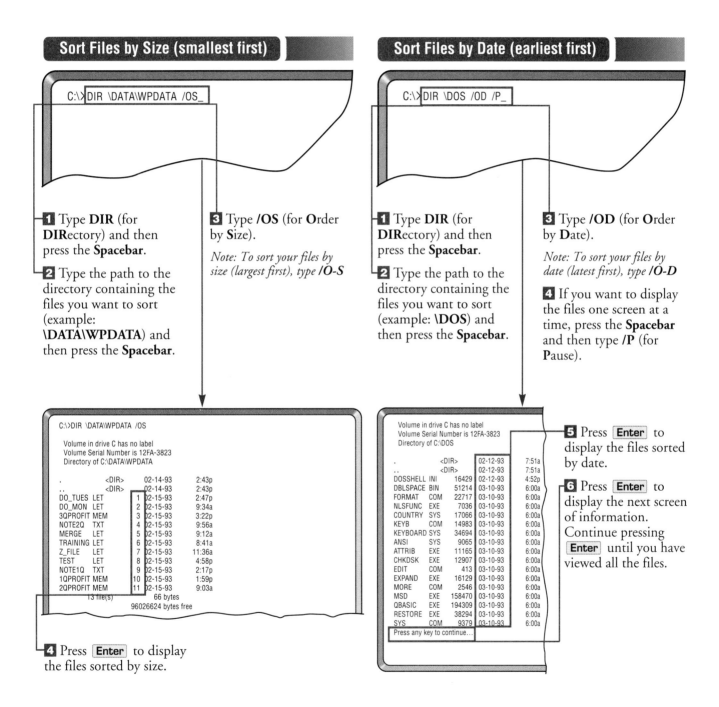

Sort Files by Size (smallest first)

C:\>DIR \DATA\WPDATA /OS_

1 Type **DIR** (for **DIR**ectory) and then press the **Spacebar**.

2 Type the path to the directory containing the files you want to sort (example: **\DATA\WPDATA**) and then press the **Spacebar**.

3 Type **/OS** (for **O**rder by **S**ize).

Note: To sort your files by size (largest first), type /O-S

```
C:\>DIR \DATA\WPDATA /OS

Volume in drive C has no label
Volume Serial Number is 12FA-3823
Directory of C:\DATA\WPDATA

.              <DIR>       02-14-93    2:43p
..             <DIR>       02-14-93    2:43p
DO_TUES  LET       1    02-15-93    2:47p
DO_MON   LET       2    02-15-93    9:34a
3QPROFIT MEM       3    02-15-93    3:22p
NOTE2Q   TXT       4    02-15-93    9:56a
MERGE    LET       5    02-15-93    9:12a
TRAINING LET       6    02-15-93    8:41a
Z_FILE   LET       7    02-15-93   11:36a
TEST     LET       8    02-15-93    4:58p
NOTE1Q   TXT       9    02-15-93    2:17p
1QPROFIT MEM      10    02-15-93    1:59p
2QPROFIT MEM      11    02-15-93    9:03a
         13 file(s)           66 bytes
                     96026624 bytes free
```

4 Press **Enter** to display the files sorted by size.

Sort Files by Date (earliest first)

C:\>DIR \DOS /OD /P_

1 Type **DIR** (for **DIR**ectory) and then press the **Spacebar**.

2 Type the path to the directory containing the files you want to sort (example: **\DOS**) and then press the **Spacebar**.

3 Type **/OD** (for **O**rder by **D**ate).

Note: To sort your files by date (latest first), type /O-D

4 If you want to display the files one screen at a time, press the **Spacebar** and then type **/P** (for **P**ause).

```
Volume in drive C has no label
Volume Serial Number is 12FA-3823
Directory of C:\DOS

.              <DIR>     02-12-93   7:51a
..             <DIR>     02-12-93   7:51a
DOSSHELL INI    16429    02-12-93   4:52p
DBLSPACE BIN    51214    03-10-93   6:00a
FORMAT   COM    22717    03-10-93   6:00a
NLSFUNC  EXE     7036    03-10-93   6:00a
COUNTRY  SYS    17066    03-10-93   6:00a
KEYB     COM    14983    03-10-93   6:00a
KEYBOARD SYS    34694    03-10-93   6:00a
ANSI     SYS     9065    03-10-93   6:00a
ATTRIB   EXE    11165    03-10-93   6:00a
CHKDSK   EXE    12907    03-10-93   6:00a
EDIT     COM      413    03-10-93   6:00a
EXPAND   EXE    16129    03-10-93   6:00a
MORE     COM     2546    03-10-93   6:00a
MSD      EXE   158470    03-10-93   6:00a
QBASIC   EXE   194309    03-10-93   6:00a
RESTORE  EXE    38294    03-10-93   6:00a
SYS      COM     9379    03-10-93   6:00a
Press any key to continue...
```

5 Press **Enter** to display the files sorted by date.

6 Press **Enter** to display the next screen of information. Continue pressing **Enter** until you have viewed all the files.

SEARCH
FOR FILES

The Search command helps you find files stored on a hard or floppy drive.

MS-DOS searches the current directory and all its subdirectories. If you want to search the entire drive, make the root directory the current directory.

Search for a File

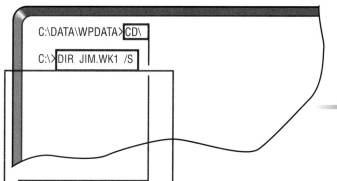

C:\DATA\WPDATA>CD\

C:\>DIR JIM.WK1 /S

1 To change to the root directory, type **CD** and then press Enter.

2 Type **DIR** (for **DIR**ectory) and then press the **Spacebar**.

3 Type the name of the file you want to search for (example: **JIM.WK1**) and then press the **Spacebar**.

4 Type **/S** (for **S**earch) and then press Enter.

Search for Files Using Wildcards

Wildcards enable you to search for several files at the same time.

In this example, MS-DOS searches for all file names starting with PLAN, with any extension.

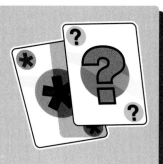

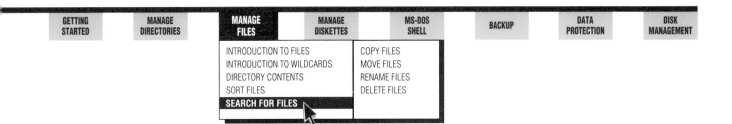

INTRODUCTION TO FILES
INTRODUCTION TO WILDCARDS
DIRECTORY CONTENTS
SORT FILES
SEARCH FOR FILES

COPY FILES
MOVE FILES
RENAME FILES
DELETE FILES

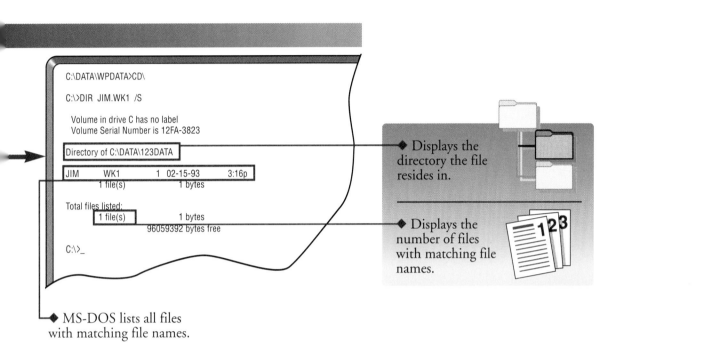

```
C:\DATA\WPDATA>CD\

C:\>DIR  JIM.WK1  /S

  Volume in drive C has no label
  Volume Serial Number is 12FA-3823

Directory of C:\DATA\123DATA

JIM      WK1        1  02-15-93     3:16p
    1 file(s)              1 bytes

Total files listed:
    1 file(s)              1 bytes
                96059392 bytes free

C:\>_
```

◆ Displays the directory the file resides in.

◆ Displays the number of files with matching file names.

◆ MS-DOS lists all files with matching file names.

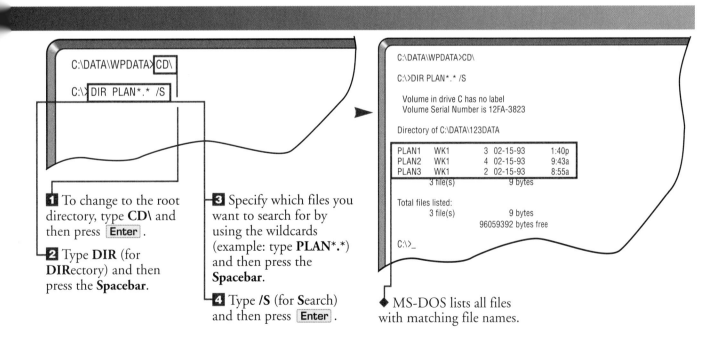

```
C:\DATA\WPDATA>CD\

C:\>DIR  PLAN*.*  /S
```

```
C:\DATA\WPDATA>CD\

C:\>DIR PLAN*.* /S

  Volume in drive C has no label
  Volume Serial Number is 12FA-3823

Directory of C:\DATA\123DATA

PLAN1    WK1        3  02-15-93     1:40p
PLAN2    WK1        4  02-15-93     9:43a
PLAN3    WK1        2  02-15-93     8:55a
    3 file(s)              9 bytes

Total files listed:
    3 file(s)              9 bytes
                96059392 bytes free

C:\>_
```

1 To change to the root directory, type **CD** and then press **Enter**.

2 Type **DIR** (for **DIR**ectory) and then press the **Spacebar**.

3 Specify which files you want to search for by using the wildcards (example: type **PLAN*.***) and then press the **Spacebar**.

4 Type **/S** (for **S**earch) and then press **Enter**.

◆ MS-DOS lists all files with matching file names.

COPY FILES

The Copy command lets you make exact copies of your files and place them in a new location.

The original files remain unaffected.

The Copy command is:

| COPY | SOURCE | DESTINATION |

SOURCE — Tells MS-DOS the location (drive and directory) and name of the file(s) you want to copy.

DESTINATION — Tells MS-DOS where (drive and directory) you want to copy the file(s). This can also tell MS-DOS the new name for the file(s).

Note: If you omit the Source drive and directory, the file(s) in the current drive and directory is copied.

If you omit the Destination drive and directory, the file(s) is copied within the current drive and directory.

It is easier to type the COPY command if you first change to the directory that contains the file(s) you want to copy.

TO CHANGE THE CURRENT DIRECTORY

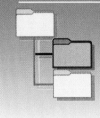

1 Type **CD** (for **C**hange **D**irectory) and then press the **Spacebar**.

2 Type the path to the directory you want to change to (example: **\DATA\WPDATA**) and then press [Enter].

COPY WITHIN THE SAME DIRECTORY

To copy a file within the same directory, you must change its name.

In this example, the MERGE.LET file is copied within the same directory and renamed MERGE.OLD.

```
C:\>CD \DATA\WPDATA

C:\DATA\WPDATA>COPY MERGE.LET MERGE.OLD
        1 file(s) copied

C:\DATA\WPDATA>_
```

1 Change to the directory that contains the file you want to copy.

2 Type **COPY** and then press the **Spacebar**.

3 Type the name of the file you want to copy (example: **MERGE.LET**) and then press the **Spacebar**.

4 Type a name for the new file (example: **MERGE.OLD**) and then press [Enter].

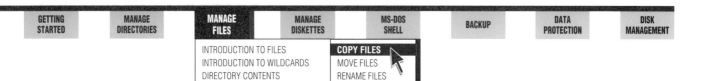

| GETTING STARTED | MANAGE DIRECTORIES | MANAGE FILES | MANAGE DISKETTES | MS-DOS SHELL | BACKUP | DATA PROTECTION | DISK MANAGEMENT |

INTRODUCTION TO FILES
INTRODUCTION TO WILDCARDS
DIRECTORY CONTENTS
SORT FILES
SEARCH FOR FILES

COPY FILES
MOVE FILES
RENAME FILES
DELETE FILES

COPY TO ANOTHER DIRECTORY

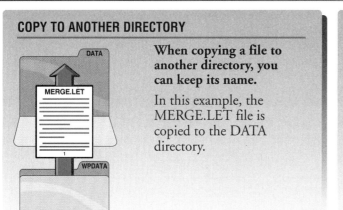

When copying a file to another directory, you can keep its name.

In this example, the MERGE.LET file is copied to the DATA directory.

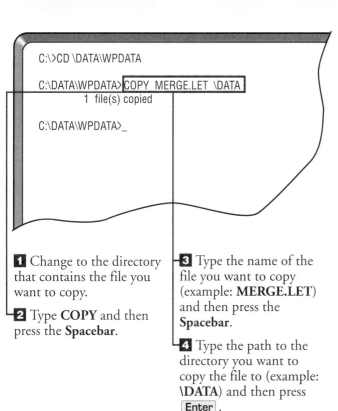

```
C:\>CD \DATA\WPDATA

C:\DATA\WPDATA> COPY MERGE.LET \DATA
        1 file(s) copied

C:\DATA\WPDATA>_
```

1 Change to the directory that contains the file you want to copy.

2 Type **COPY** and then press the **Spacebar**.

3 Type the name of the file you want to copy (example: **MERGE.LET**) and then press the **Spacebar**.

4 Type the path to the directory you want to copy the file to (example: **\DATA**) and then press Enter.

COPY USING WILDCARDS

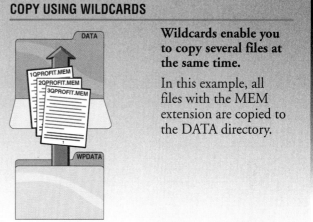

Wildcards enable you to copy several files at the same time.

In this example, all files with the MEM extension are copied to the DATA directory.

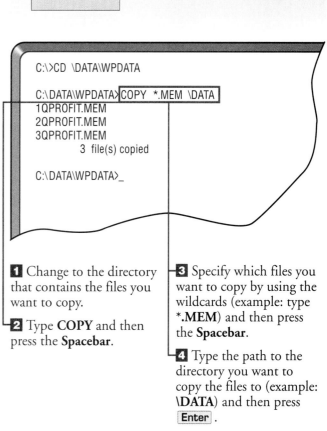

```
C:\>CD \DATA\WPDATA

C:\DATA\WPDATA> COPY *.MEM \DATA
1QPROFIT.MEM
2QPROFIT.MEM
3QPROFIT.MEM
        3 file(s) copied

C:\DATA\WPDATA>_
```

1 Change to the directory that contains the files you want to copy.

2 Type **COPY** and then press the **Spacebar**.

3 Specify which files you want to copy by using the wildcards (example: type *.**MEM**) and then press the **Spacebar**.

4 Type the path to the directory you want to copy the files to (example: **\DATA**) and then press Enter.

COPY FILES

Before copying files to a floppy drive, make sure you insert a formatted diskette into the drive.

COPY USING THE SAME NAME

In this example, the MERGE.LET file is copied to a diskette.

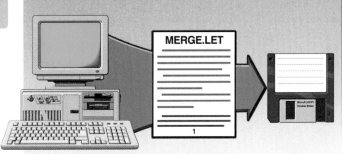

MERGE.LET

THE DRIVE NAME

B: = **"B drive"**   ◆ The drive name consists of two parts: the letter and a colon (:). The colon represents the word "drive." For example, typing **B:** refers to the **B drive**.

```
C:\>CD \DATA\WPDATA

C:\DATA\WPDATA>COPY MERGE.LET B:\
         1 file(s) copied

C:\DATA\WPDATA>_
```

1 Change to the directory that contains the file you want to copy.

2 Type **COPY** and then press the **Spacebar**.

3 Type the name of the file you want to copy (example: **MERGE.LET**) and then press the **Spacebar**.

4 Type the drive name, then type the path to the directory you want to copy the file to (example: **B:**). Then press **Enter**.

Note: The \ stands for the root directory of the drive.

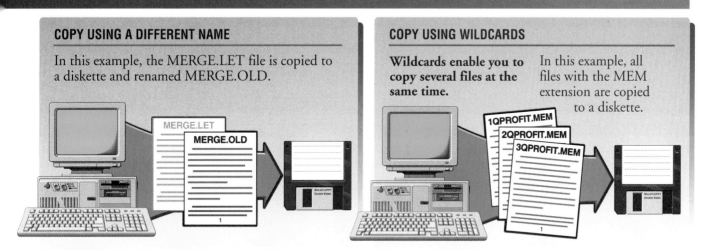

INTRODUCTION TO FILES
INTRODUCTION TO WILDCARDS
DIRECTORY CONTENTS
SORT FILES
SEARCH FOR FILES

COPY FILES
MOVE FILES
RENAME FILES
DELETE FILES

COPY USING A DIFFERENT NAME

In this example, the MERGE.LET file is copied to a diskette and renamed MERGE.OLD.

MERGE.LET
MERGE.OLD

COPY USING WILDCARDS

Wildcards enable you to copy several files at the same time. In this example, all files with the MEM extension are copied to a diskette.

1QPROFIT.MEM
2QPROFIT.MEM
3QPROFIT.MEM

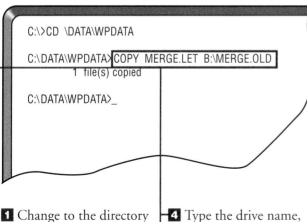

```
C:\>CD \DATA\WPDATA

C:\DATA\WPDATA>COPY MERGE.LET B:\MERGE.OLD
        1 file(s) copied

C:\DATA\WPDATA>_
```

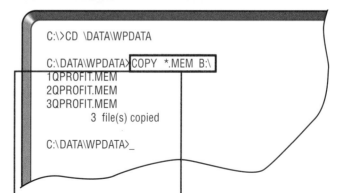

```
C:\>CD \DATA\WPDATA

C:\DATA\WPDATA>COPY *.MEM B:\
1QPROFIT.MEM
2QPROFIT.MEM
3QPROFIT.MEM
        3 file(s) copied

C:\DATA\WPDATA>_
```

1 Change to the directory that contains the file you want to copy.

2 Type **COPY** and then press the **Spacebar**.

3 Type the name of the file you want to copy (example: **MERGE.LET**) and then press the **Spacebar**.

4 Type the drive name, then type the path to the directory you want to copy the file to (example: **B:**).

Note: The \ stands for the root directory of the drive.

5 Type a name for the new file (example: **MERGE.OLD**) and then press **Enter**.

1 Change to the directory that contains the files you want to copy.

2 Type **COPY** and then press the **Spacebar**.

3 Specify which files you want to copy by using the wildcards (example: type *.**MEM**) and then press the **Spacebar**.

4 Type the drive name, then type the path to the directory you want to copy the files to (example: **B:**). Then press **Enter**.

Note: The \ stands for the root directory of the drive.

MOVE FILES

The Move command lets you remove your files from one location and place them in another.

The Move command is:		
MOVE	**SOURCE**	**DESTINATION**

SOURCE	Tells MS-DOS the location (drive and directory) and name of the file(s) you want to move.
DESTINATION	Tells MS-DOS where (drive and directory) you want to move the file(s). This can also tell MS-DOS the new name for the file(s).

Note: If you omit the Source drive and directory, the file(s) in the current drive and directory is moved.

If you omit the Destination drive, the file(s) is moved within the current drive.

It is easier to type the MOVE command if you first change to the directory that contains the file(s) you want to move.

Move Files

MOVE TO A DIFFERENT DIRECTORY

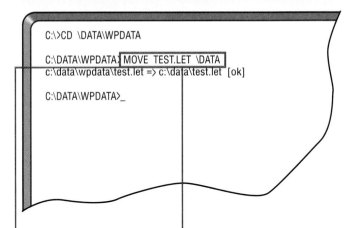

In this example, the TEST.LET file is moved to the DATA directory.

```
C:\>CD \DATA\WPDATA

C:\DATA\WPDATA> MOVE TEST.LET \DATA
c:\data\wpdata\test.let => c:\data\test.let [ok]

C:\DATA\WPDATA>_
```

1 Change to the directory that contains the file you want to move.

2 Type **MOVE** and then press the **Spacebar**.

3 Type the name of the file you want to move (example: **TEST.LET**) and then press the **Spacebar**.

4 Type the path to the directory you want to move the file to (example: **\DATA**) and then press Enter .

| GETTING STARTED | MANAGE DIRECTORIES | MANAGE FILES | | MANAGE DISKETTES | | MS-DOS SHELL | BACKUP | DATA PROTECTION | DISK MANAGEMENT |

INTRODUCTION TO FILES   COPY FILES
INTRODUCTION TO WILDCARDS   **MOVE FILES**
DIRECTORY CONTENTS   RENAME FILES
SORT FILES   DELETE FILES
SEARCH FOR FILES

MOVE TO A DIFFERENT DRIVE

In this example, the TRAINING.LET file is moved to a diskette.

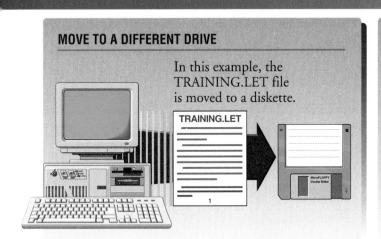

MOVE USING WILDCARDS

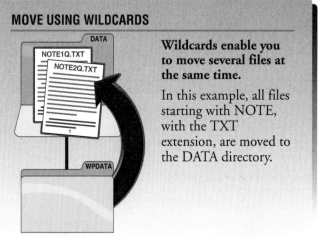

Wildcards enable you to move several files at the same time.

In this example, all files starting with NOTE, with the TXT extension, are moved to the DATA directory.

```
C:\>CD \DATA\WPDATA

C:\DATA\WPDATA>MOVE TRAINING.LET B:\
c:\data\wpdata\training.let => b:\training.let  [ok]

C:\DATA\WPDATA>_
```

```
C:\>CD \DATA\WPDATA

C:\DATA\WPDATA>MOVE NOTE*.TXT \DATA
c:\data\wpdata\note1q.txt => c:\data\note1q.txt  [ok]
c:\data\wpdata\note2q.txt => c:\data\note2q.txt  [ok]

C:\DATA\WPDATA>_
```

1 Change to the directory that contains the file you want to move.

2 Type **MOVE** and then press the **Spacebar**.

3 Type the name of the file you want to move (example: **TRAINING.LET**) and then press the **Spacebar**.

4 Type the drive name, then type the path to the directory you want to move the file to (example: **B:**). Then press **Enter** .

Note: The **** *stands for the root directory of the drive.*

1 Change to the directory that contains the files you want to move.

2 Type **MOVE** and then press the **Spacebar**.

3 Specify which files you want to move by using the wildcards (example: type **NOTE*.TXT**) and then press the **Spacebar**.

4 Type the path to the directory you want to move the files to (example: **\DATA**) and then press **Enter** .

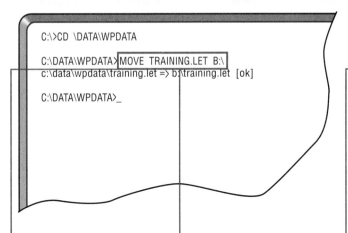

45

RENAME FILES

The Rename command lets you change the name of one or more files.

The Rename command is:

| RENAME | DRIVE | PATH | FILENAME1 | FILENAME2 |

DRIVE	Tells MS-DOS the drive containing the file(s) you want to rename.
PATH	Tells MS-DOS the path to the directory containing the file(s) you want to rename.
FILENAME1	Tells MS-DOS the name of the file(s) you want to rename.
FILENAME2	Tells MS-DOS the new name for the file(s).

Note: If you omit the drive and path, MS-DOS renames the file(s) in the current drive and directory.

It is easier to type the RENAME command if you first change to the directory that contains the file(s) you want to rename.

IMPORTANT!

Since every file in a directory must have a unique name, you cannot rename a file using a file name that already exists.

Rename a File

In this example, the DO_TUES.LET file is renamed DO_WED.TXT.

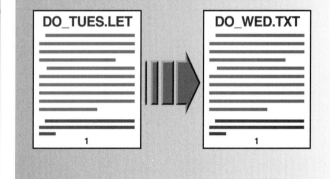

DO_TUES.LET → DO_WED.TXT

Rename Files Using Wildcards

Wildcards enable you to rename several files at the same time.

In this example, all files with the MEM extension are renamed with the OLD extension.

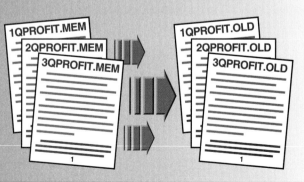

1QPROFIT.MEM → 1QPROFIT.OLD
2QPROFIT.MEM → 2QPROFIT.OLD
3QPROFIT.MEM → 3QPROFIT.OLD

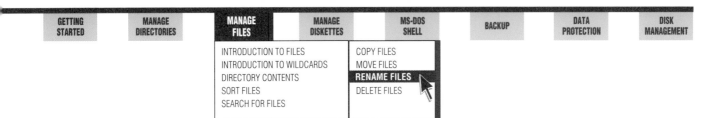

| GETTING STARTED | MANAGE DIRECTORIES | **MANAGE FILES** | MANAGE DISKETTES | MS-DOS SHELL | BACKUP | DATA PROTECTION | DISK MANAGEMENT |

INTRODUCTION TO FILES
INTRODUCTION TO WILDCARDS
DIRECTORY CONTENTS
SORT FILES
SEARCH FOR FILES

COPY FILES
MOVE FILES
RENAME FILES
DELETE FILES

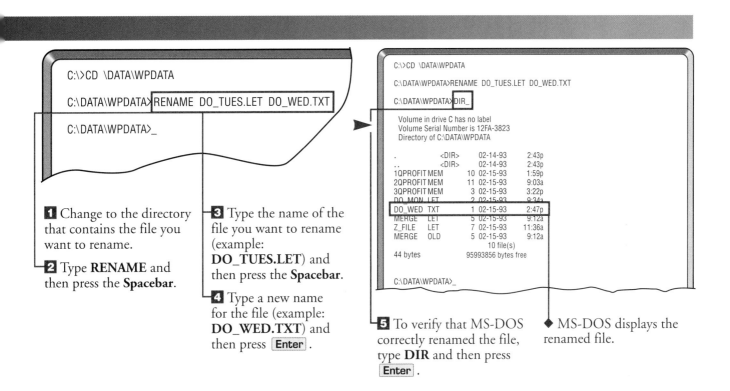

```
C:\>CD \DATA\WPDATA

C:\DATA\WPDATA>RENAME  DO_TUES.LET  DO_WED.TXT

C:\DATA\WPDATA>_
```

```
C:\>CD \DATA\WPDATA

C:\DATA\WPDATA>RENAME  DO_TUES.LET  DO_WED.TXT

C:\DATA\WPDATA>DIR_

   Volume in drive C has no label
   Volume Serial Number is 12FA-3823
   Directory of C:\DATA\WPDATA

.              <DIR>        02-14-93    2:43p
..             <DIR>        02-14-93    2:43p
1QPROFIT MEM        10  02-15-93    1:59p
2QPROFIT MEM        11  02-15-93    9:03a
3QPROFIT MEM         3  02-15-93    3:22p
DO_MON  LET          2  02-15-93    9:34a
DO_WED  TXT          1  02-15-93    2:47p
MERGE   LET          5  02-15-93    9:12a
Z_FILE  LET          7  02-15-93   11:36a
MERGE   OLD          5  02-15-93    9:12a
                          10 file(s)
   44 bytes           95993856 bytes free


C:\DATA\WPDATA>_
```

1 Change to the directory that contains the file you want to rename.

2 Type **RENAME** and then press the **Spacebar**.

3 Type the name of the file you want to rename (example: **DO_TUES.LET**) and then press the **Spacebar**.

4 Type a new name for the file (example: **DO_WED.TXT**) and then press **Enter**.

5 To verify that MS-DOS correctly renamed the file, type **DIR** and then press **Enter**.

◆ MS-DOS displays the renamed file.

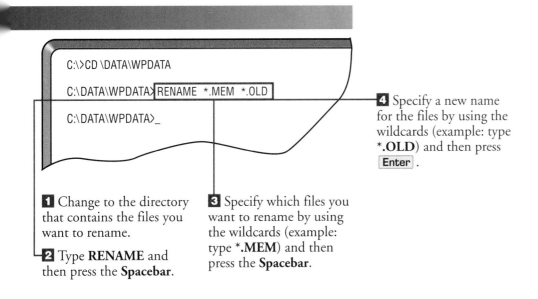

```
C:\>CD \DATA\WPDATA

C:\DATA\WPDATA>RENAME  *.MEM  *.OLD

C:\DATA\WPDATA>_
```

1 Change to the directory that contains the files you want to rename.

2 Type **RENAME** and then press the **Spacebar**.

3 Specify which files you want to rename by using the wildcards (example: type *.MEM) and then press the **Spacebar**.

4 Specify a new name for the files by using the wildcards (example: type *.OLD) and then press **Enter**.

DELETE FILES

The Delete command (typed as DEL) lets you erase files that you no longer require.

The Delete command is:

DEL	DRIVE	PATH	FILENAME	/P

DEL	Stands for DELete.
DRIVE	Tells MS-DOS the drive containing the file(s) you want to delete.
PATH	Tells MS-DOS the path to the directory containing the file(s) you want to delete.
FILENAME	Tells MS-DOS the name of the file(s) you want to delete.
/P	Tells MS-DOS to ask you for confirmation before deleting a file.

Note: If you omit the drive and path, MS-DOS deletes the file(s) in the current drive and directory.

It is easier to type the DELETE command if you first change to the directory that contains the file(s) you want to delete.

You can use Delete Sentry to fully recover deleted files. For more information, refer to page 98.

Delete a File

In this example, the DO_MON.LET file is deleted.

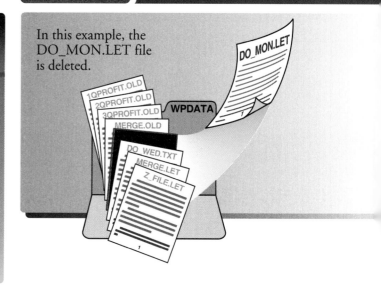

Delete Files Using Wildcards

Wildcards enable you to delete several files at the same time.

In this example, all files with the OLD extension are deleted.

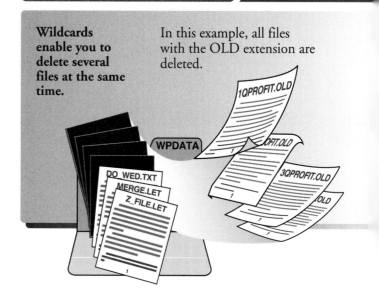

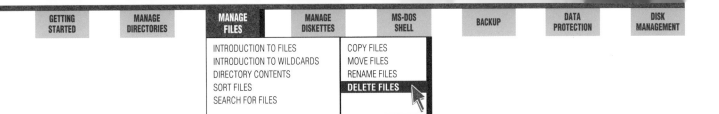

| GETTING STARTED | MANAGE DIRECTORIES | **MANAGE FILES** | MANAGE DISKETTES | MS-DOS SHELL | BACKUP | DATA PROTECTION | DISK MANAGEMENT |

INTRODUCTION TO FILES
INTRODUCTION TO WILDCARDS
DIRECTORY CONTENTS
SORT FILES
SEARCH FOR FILES

COPY FILES
MOVE FILES
RENAME FILES
DELETE FILES

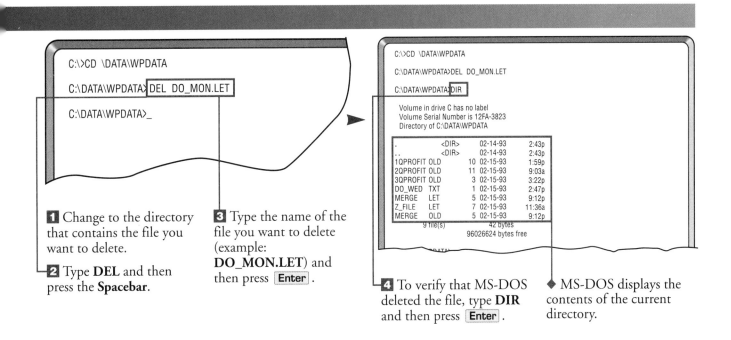

1 Change to the directory that contains the file you want to delete.

2 Type **DEL** and then press the **Spacebar**.

3 Type the name of the file you want to delete (example: **DO_MON.LET**) and then press **Enter**.

4 To verify that MS-DOS deleted the file, type **DIR** and then press **Enter**.

◆ MS-DOS displays the contents of the current directory.

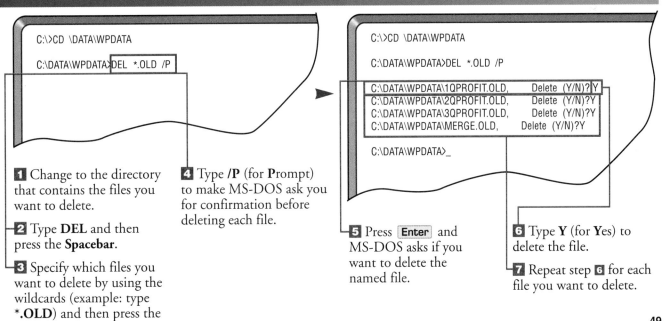

1 Change to the directory that contains the files you want to delete.

2 Type **DEL** and then press the **Spacebar**.

3 Specify which files you want to delete by using the wildcards (example: type ***.OLD**) and then press the **Spacebar**.

4 Type **/P** (for **P**rompt) to make MS-DOS ask you for confirmation before deleting each file.

5 Press **Enter** and MS-DOS asks if you want to delete the named file.

6 Type **Y** (for **Y**es) to delete the file.

7 Repeat step **6** for each file you want to delete.

49

INTRODUCTION TO DISKETTES

Diskettes

You can store programs and data on diskettes (or floppy disks). Diskettes are commonly used to transfer information from one computer to another or to make a backup copy of a hard drive's contents.

5.25" DISKETTE

◆ Most diskettes have a label to describe their contents. Use a soft-tipped felt marker to write on the label. A pen or pencil may damage the diskette.

◆ You can "write-protect" a diskette to prevent erasing or recording information on it. To write-protect a 5.25" diskette, place a small sticker over the notch on the diskette.

Not Write-Protected   **Write-Protected**

3.5" DISKETTE

MicroFLOPPY
Double Sided

◆ A 3.5" diskette has a write-protect tab. You can only record and erase data on the diskette when the tab is in the "Not Write-Protected" position.

Not Write-Protected   **Write-Protected**

INTRODUCTION TO DISKETTES
FORMAT
DISKCOPY

Diskette Capacity

The capacity of a diskette tells you how much information a diskette can store.

If a typed page contains 1,000 characters (approximately 1K), then a 720K diskette can store 720 pages of information.

Note: 1,000K equals 1MB.

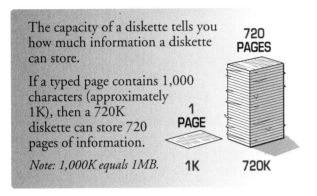

720 PAGES

1 PAGE

1K   **720K**

5.25 and 3.5 inch diskettes offer two types of storage capacities.

◆ A "high-density" diskette can store more information than a "double-density" diskette of the same size.

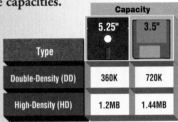

	Capacity 5.25"	3.5"
Type		
Double-Density (DD)	360K	720K
High-Density (HD)	1.2MB	1.44MB

Floppy Drives

Floppy drives store programs and data onto diskettes.

5.25" FLOPPY DRIVE

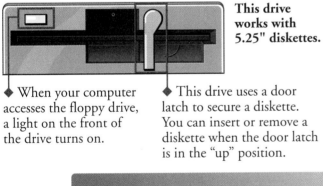

This drive works with 5.25" diskettes.

◆ When your computer accesses the floppy drive, a light on the front of the drive turns on.

◆ This drive uses a door latch to secure a diskette. You can insert or remove a diskette when the door latch is in the "up" position.

3.5" FLOPPY DRIVE

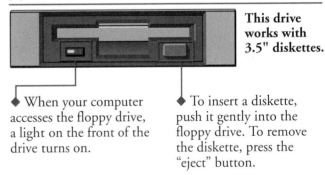

This drive works with 3.5" diskettes.

◆ When your computer accesses the floppy drive, a light on the front of the drive turns on.

◆ To insert a diskette, push it gently into the floppy drive. To remove the diskette, press the "eject" button.

This chart shows the types of diskettes you can use with double-density and high-density drives.

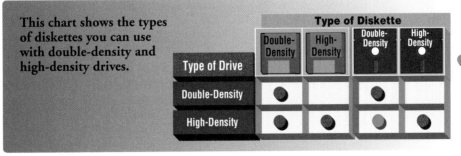

Type of Drive	Type of Diskette Double-Density	High-Density	Double-Density	High-Density
Double-Density	●		●	
High-Density	●	●	●	●

● A high-density drive can read a 5.25" double-density diskette, but should not be used to write to it.

FORMAT

Format a Diskette

You must format a diskette before storing data on it. Formatting prepares the diskette for use.

```
C:\>FORMAT B:
Insert new diskette for drive B:
and press ENTER when ready... _
```

1 Type **FORMAT** and then press the **Spacebar**.

2 Type the name of the drive that contains the diskette you want to format (example: **B:**) and then press Enter.

3 Insert the diskette into the drive and then press Enter.

The Format command is:

FORMAT DRIVE

DRIVE   Tells MS-DOS which drive contains the diskette you want to format.

THE DRIVE NAME

B: = "B drive"   To indicate which drive contains the diskette you want to format, type a colon (:) after the drive letter. The colon represents the word "drive." For example, typing **B:** refers to the **B drive**.

◆ The Format command erases all the information on a diskette. Do not format a diskette containing information you want to retain.

◆ If you accidentally format a diskette, it may be possible to recover all of its files by using the Unformat command. Refer to your Microsoft User's Guide or check with a computer expert.

CAUTION

| GETTING STARTED | MANAGE DIRECTORIES | MANAGE FILES | MANAGE DISKETTES | MS-DOS SHELL | BACKUP | DATA PROTECTION | DISK MANAGEMENT |

INTRODUCTION TO DISKETTES
FORMAT
DISKCOPY

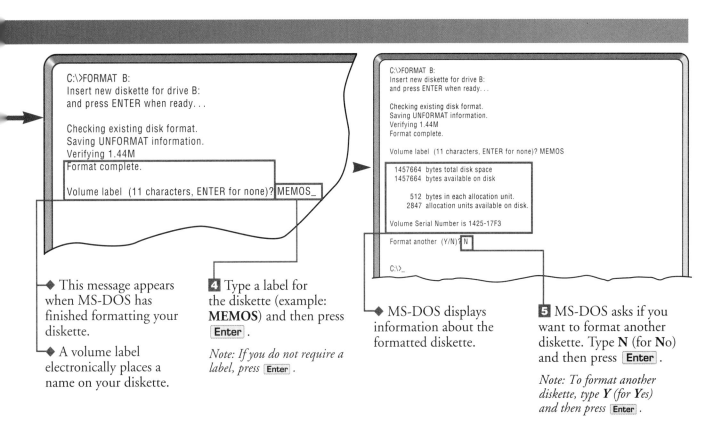

```
C:\>FORMAT B:
Insert new diskette for drive B:
and press ENTER when ready. . .

Checking existing disk format.
Saving UNFORMAT information.
Verifying 1.44M
Format complete.

Volume label  (11 characters, ENTER for none)? MEMOS_
```

```
C:\>FORMAT B:
Insert new diskette for drive B:
and press ENTER when ready. . .

Checking existing disk format.
Saving UNFORMAT information.
Verifying 1.44M
Format complete.

Volume label  (11 characters, ENTER for none)? MEMOS

 1457664  bytes total disk space
 1457664  bytes available on disk

     512  bytes in each allocation unit.
    2847  allocation units available on disk.

Volume Serial Number is 1425-17F3

Format another  (Y/N)? N

C:\>_
```

◆ This message appears when MS-DOS has finished formatting your diskette.

◆ A volume label electronically places a name on your diskette.

4 Type a label for the diskette (example: **MEMOS**) and then press **Enter** .

Note: If you do not require a label, press **Enter** .

◆ MS-DOS displays information about the formatted diskette.

5 MS-DOS asks if you want to format another diskette. Type **N** (for **N**o) and then press **Enter** .

Note: To format another diskette, type **Y** *(for* **Y***es) and then press* **Enter** .

Display a Volume Label

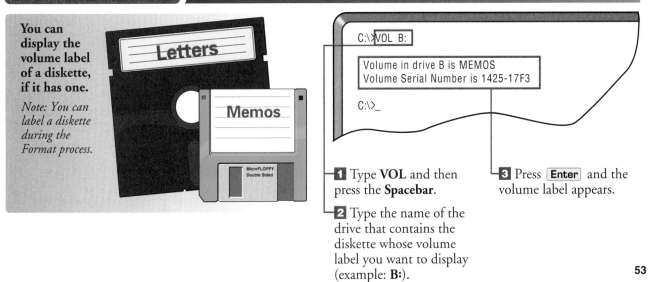

You can display the volume label of a diskette, if it has one.

Note: You can label a diskette during the Format process.

Letters

Memos

MicroFLOPPY
Double Sided

```
C:\>VOL B:

Volume in drive B is MEMOS
Volume Serial Number is 1425-17F3

C:\>_
```

1 Type **VOL** and then press the **Spacebar**.

2 Type the name of the drive that contains the diskette whose volume label you want to display (example: **B:**).

3 Press **Enter** and the volume label appears.

DISKCOPY

The Diskcopy command lets you copy the entire contents of one diskette to another. The second diskette becomes an exact copy of the first one.

SOURCE DISKETTE

Copy a Disk

The Diskcopy command is:

DISKCOPY | **SOURCE** | **TARGET**

SOURCE   Tells MS-DOS which drive you want to copy the files from.

TARGET   Tells MS-DOS which drive you want to copy the files to.

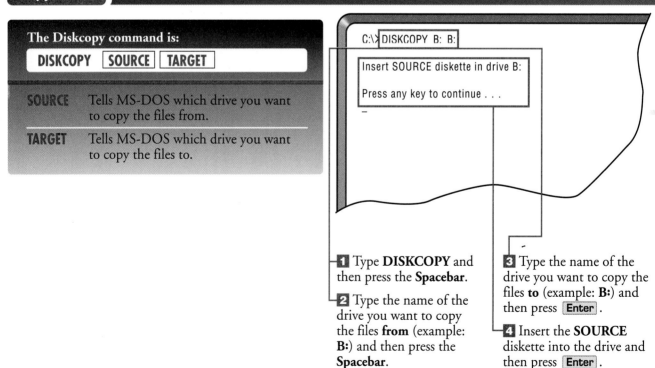

```
C:\> DISKCOPY B: B:
Insert SOURCE diskette in drive B:
Press any key to continue . . .
_
```

1 Type **DISKCOPY** and then press the **Spacebar**.

2 Type the name of the drive you want to copy the files **from** (example: **B:**) and then press the **Spacebar**.

3 Type the name of the drive you want to copy the files **to** (example: **B:**) and then press **Enter**.

4 Insert the **SOURCE** diskette into the drive and then press **Enter**.

INTRODUCTION TO DISKETTES
FORMAT
DISKCOPY

Note: The source and target diskettes must be the same size and capacity.

TARGET DISKETTE

The Diskcopy command automatically formats the target diskette during the copy process. Its contents are completely destroyed, so make sure it does not contain any files you want to keep.

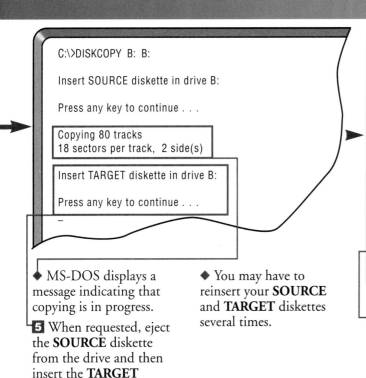

```
C:\>DISKCOPY B: B:

Insert SOURCE diskette in drive B:

Press any key to continue . . .

Copying 80 tracks
18 sectors per track,  2 side(s)

Insert TARGET diskette in drive B:

Press any key to continue . . .
_
```

```
Insert TARGET diskette in drive B:

Press any key to continue . . .

Insert SOURCE diskette in drive B:

Press any key to continue . . .

Insert TARGET diskette in drive B:

Press any key to continue . . .

Insert SOURCE diskette in drive B:

Press any key to continue . . .

Insert TARGET diskette in drive B:

Press any key to continue . . .

Volume Serial Number is 1425-17F3

Copy another diskette  (Y/N)? N

C:\>_
```

*Note: To copy another diskette, type **Y** (for **Y**es).*

◆ MS-DOS displays a message indicating that copying is in progress.

5 When requested, eject the **SOURCE** diskette from the drive and then insert the **TARGET** diskette. Press `Enter`.

◆ You may have to reinsert your **SOURCE** and **TARGET** diskettes several times.

6 When MS-DOS has finished copying the diskette, it asks if you want to copy another one. Type **N** (for **N**o).

START THE
MS-DOS SHELL

1 To start the MS-DOS Shell, type **DOSSHELL** and then press Enter.

`C:\>DOSSHELL_`

KEY COMBINATIONS

◆ If key names are separated by a plus (+) sign, press and hold down the first key before pressing the second key (example: Shift + Tab).

◆ If key names are separated by a comma (,), press and release the first key before pressing the second key (example: Alt , F).

GETTING STARTED	MANAGE DIRECTORIES	MANAGE FILES	MANAGE DISKETTES	MS-DOS SHELL		BACKUP	DATA PROTECTION	DISK MANAGEMENT

GETTING STARTED ▶   **START THE MS-DOS SHELL**
MANAGE DIRECTORIES ▶   MOUSE BASICS
MANAGE FILES   ▶   SELECT COMMANDS
                CHANGE SCREEN DISPLAY AND COLORS
                HELP

The MS-DOS Shell

The **Drive** area displays the drives in your computer. The current drive is highlighted (example: drive **C**).

The **Directory Tree** area displays the directories in the current drive. The current directory is highlighted (example: **C:**).

The MS-DOS Shell provides an easy, graphic approach to using most commands.

```
MS–DOS Shell
File  Options  View  Tree  Help
C:\
[🖳]A  [🖳]B  [💽]C
```

```
┌──── Directory Tree ────┐  ┌──────── C:\*.* ────────┐
│ [−] C:\              ↑ │  │ 📄 AUTOEXEC.BAT   127   03-18-93 ↑ │
│     ├─🗀 123           │  │ 📄 COMMAND.COM 52,925  02-12-93   │
│     ├─🗀 DATA          │  │ 📄 CONFIG  .SYS   135   03-18-93  │
│     ├─🗀 DOS           │  │ 📄 WINA20  .386  9,349  02-12-93  │
│     └─🗀 WP            │  │                                  │
│                     ↓ │  │                              ↓   │
└───────────────────────┘  └──────────────────────────────┘
```

```
┌──────────────── Main ────────────────┐
│ 🗀 Command Prompt                  ↑ │
│ 🗀 Editor                            │
│ 🗀 MS-DOS QBasic                     │
│ ▦ Disk Utilities                    │
│                                   ↓ │
└───────────────────────────────────────┘
F10=Actions   Shift+F9=Command Prompt            4:07p
```

The **File** area lists all the files in the current directory.

The **Main** area lists the programs and utilities installed in your computer.

If the **Main** area is not displayed, press `Alt`, `V`, `F` to display it.

Note: If the graphics in the above screen do not match your display, refer to "Change Screen Display and Colors" on page 62.

SELECT AN AREA

◆ To move from one area to another, press `Tab`. The MS-DOS Shell highlights the bar above the selected area.

◆ To move in the opposite direction, press `Shift` + `Tab`.

Using the Mouse

● Move the pointer ⬉ anywhere in the area you want to select and then click the left mouse button.

MOUSE BASICS

Using a Mouse

With MS-DOS, you can use a mouse to replace hard-to-remember key combinations with easy "point and click" actions.

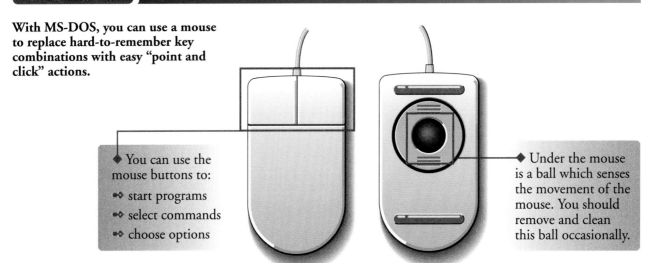

◆ You can use the mouse buttons to:

•❖ start programs

•❖ select commands

•❖ choose options

◆ Under the mouse is a ball which senses the movement of the mouse. You should remove and clean this ball occasionally.

Holding the Mouse

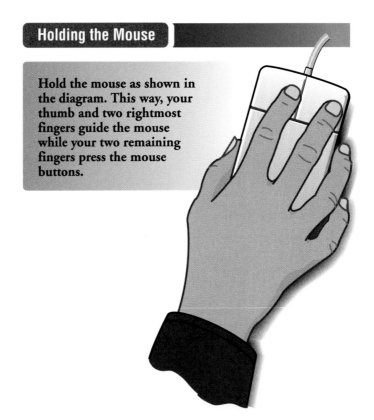

Hold the mouse as shown in the diagram. This way, your thumb and two rightmost fingers guide the mouse while your two remaining fingers press the mouse buttons.

GETTING STARTED ▶
MANAGE DIRECTORIES ▶
MANAGE FILES ▶

START THE MS-DOS SHELL
MOUSE BASICS
SELECT COMMANDS
CHANGE SCREEN DISPLAY AND COLORS
HELP

Moving the Mouse Pointer

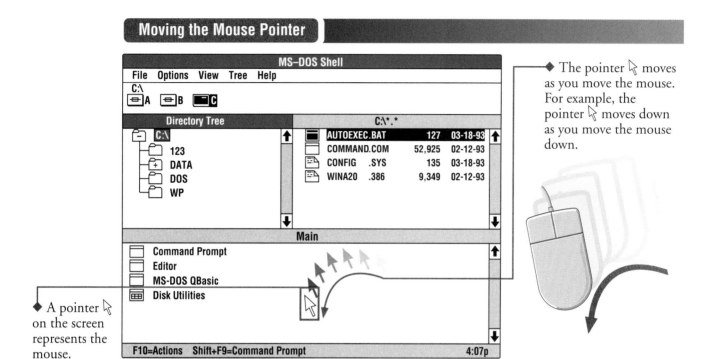

◆ The pointer ⬎ moves as you move the mouse. For example, the pointer ⬎ moves down as you move the mouse down.

◆ A pointer ⬎ on the screen represents the mouse.

Common Mouse Terms

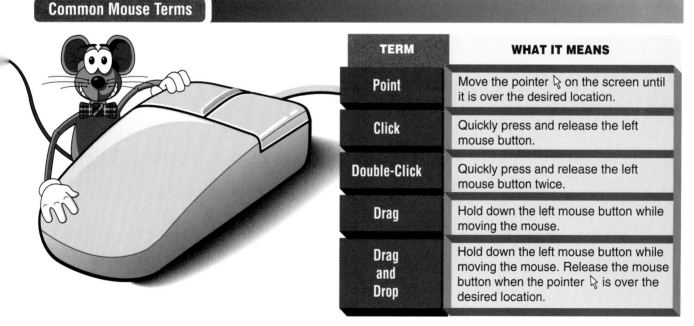

TERM	WHAT IT MEANS
Point	Move the pointer ⬎ on the screen until it is over the desired location.
Click	Quickly press and release the left mouse button.
Double-Click	Quickly press and release the left mouse button twice.
Drag	Hold down the left mouse button while moving the mouse.
Drag and Drop	Hold down the left mouse button while moving the mouse. Release the mouse button when the pointer ⬎ is over the desired location.

SELECT COMMANDS

The MS-DOS Shell Menu Bar is similar to a restaurant menu. They both offer a list of options you can choose from.

In the MS-DOS Shell Menu Bar, you can pull down each menu to display a list of commands.

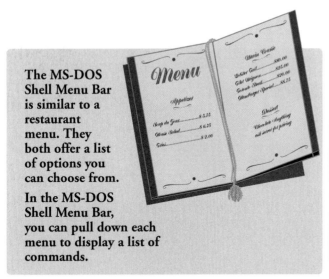

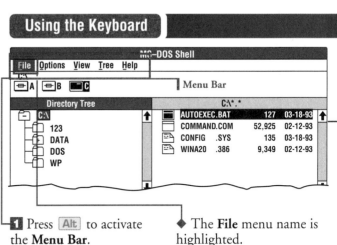

1 Press **Alt** to activate the **Menu Bar**.

◆ The **File** menu name is highlighted.

Using the Mouse

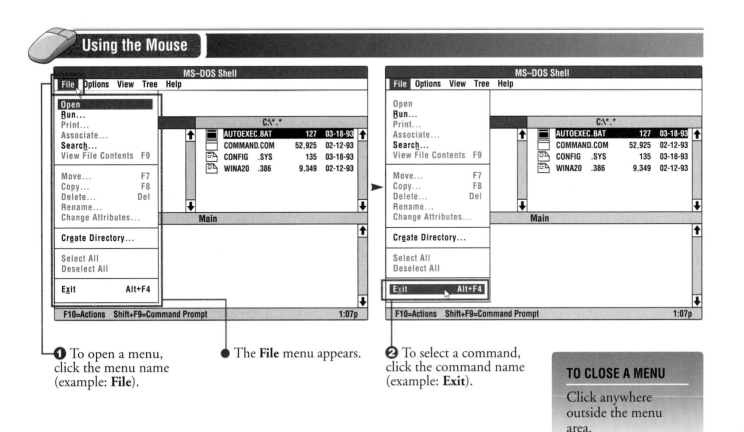

1 To open a menu, click the menu name (example: **File**).

● The **File** menu appears.

2 To select a command, click the command name (example: **Exit**).

TO CLOSE A MENU

Click anywhere outside the menu area.

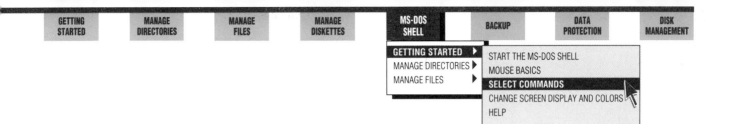

GETTING STARTED ▶   START THE MS-DOS SHELL
MANAGE DIRECTORIES ▶   MOUSE BASICS
MANAGE FILES ▶   **SELECT COMMANDS**
   CHANGE SCREEN DISPLAY AND COLORS
   HELP

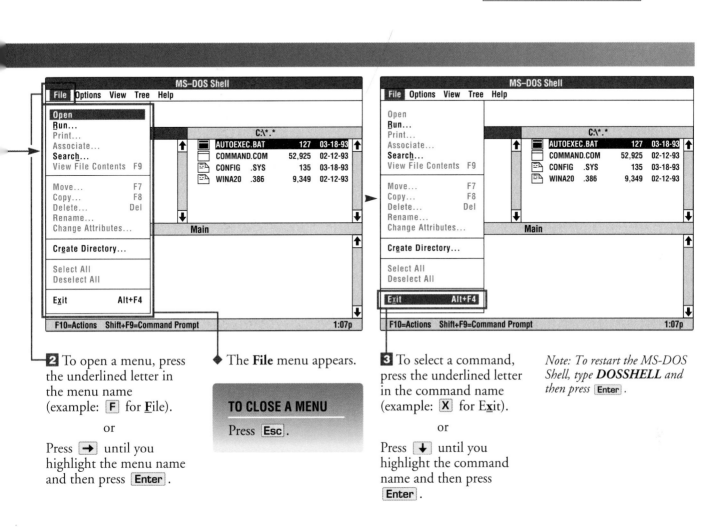

2 To open a menu, press the underlined letter in the menu name (example: **F** for **F**ile).

or

Press **→** until you highlight the menu name and then press **Enter**.

◆ The **File** menu appears.

TO CLOSE A MENU

Press **Esc**.

3 To select a command, press the underlined letter in the command name (example: **X** for E**x**it).

or

Press **↓** until you highlight the command name and then press **Enter**.

*Note: To restart the MS-DOS Shell, type **DOSSHELL** and then press **Enter**.*

CHANGE SCREEN DISPLAY AND COLORS

Change Screen Display

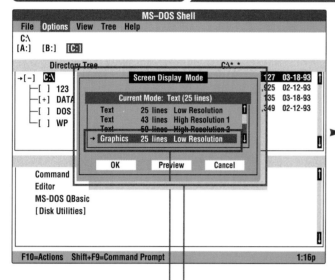

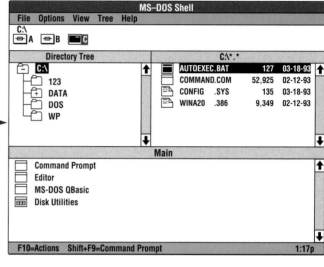

When you first start the MS-DOS Shell, the above screen appears.

If your computer has color graphics capability, you can change its screen display and colors.

1 Press `Alt`, `O`, `D` and the **Screen Display Mode** dialog box appears.

2 Press `↓` or `↑` until you highlight the desired screen display mode and then press `Enter`.

◆ The new screen display mode appears (example: **Graphics 25 lines Low Resolution**).

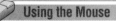 **Using the Mouse**

❶ Click **Options** to open its menu.

❷ Click **Display** and the **Screen Display Mode** dialog box appears.

❸ Click the desired screen display mode.

❹ Click the **OK** button.

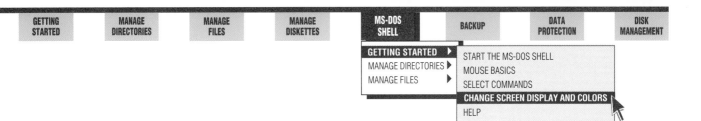

| GETTING STARTED | MANAGE DIRECTORIES | MANAGE FILES | MANAGE DISKETTES | MS-DOS SHELL | | BACKUP | DATA PROTECTION | DISK MANAGEMENT |

GETTING STARTED ▶ | START THE MS-DOS SHELL
MANAGE DIRECTORIES ▶ | MOUSE BASICS
MANAGE FILES ▶ | SELECT COMMANDS
| **CHANGE SCREEN DISPLAY AND COLORS** ▶
| HELP

Change Screen Colors

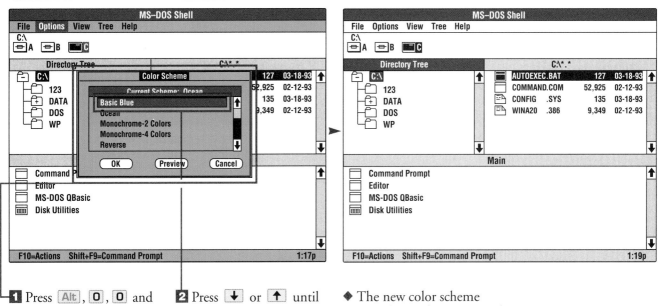

▌1 Press Alt, O, O and the **Color Scheme** dialog box appears.

▌2 Press ↓ or ↑ until you highlight the desired color scheme and then press Enter.

◆ The new color scheme appears (example: **Basic Blue**).

Using the Mouse

❶ Click **Options** to open its menu.

❷ Click **Colors** and the **Color Scheme** dialog box appears.

❸ Click the desired color scheme.

❹ Click the **OK** button.

The MS-DOS Shell offers a variety of screen colors. Some examples are:

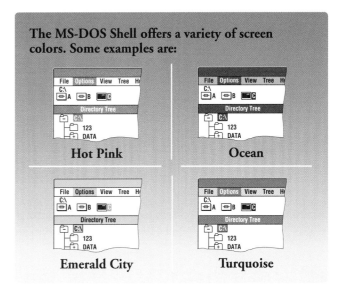

Hot Pink   Ocean

Emerald City   Turquoise

63

HELP

Getting Help on Commands and Procedures

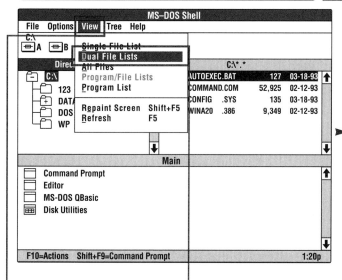

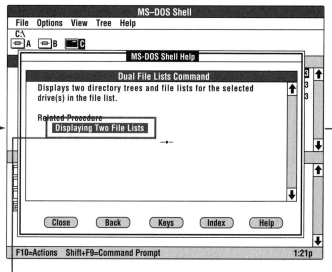

Help information is available for all commands listed in each menu.

1 Press `Alt` to activate the **Menu Bar**.

2 To open a menu, press the underlined letter in the menu name (example: `V` for **V**iew).

3 Press `↓` until you highlight the command you want help on (example: **Dual File Lists**).

4 Press `F1` and help information appears.

5 To display help information on a highlighted procedure (example: **Displaying Two File Lists**), press `Enter`.

Note: Some Help screens display more than one related procedure. To receive help on another procedure, press `Tab` until you highlight it and then press `Enter`.

TO CANCEL HELP

Press `Esc`.

Using the Mouse

❶ To open a menu, click the menu name (example: **View**).

❷ Press `↓` until you highlight the command you want help on (example: **Dual File Lists**).

❸ Press `F1` and help information appears.

❹ Double-click a related procedure you want to display help information on (example: **Displaying Two File Lists**).

TO CANCEL HELP

Click `Close`.

GETTING STARTED	MANAGE DIRECTORIES	MANAGE FILES	MANAGE DISKETTES	MS-DOS SHELL	BACKUP	DATA PROTECTION	DISK MANAGEMENT

GETTING STARTED ▶   START THE MS-DOS SHELL
MANAGE DIRECTORIES ▶   MOUSE BASICS
MANAGE FILES   ▶   SELECT COMMANDS
                                 CHANGE SCREEN DISPLAY AND COLORS
HELP

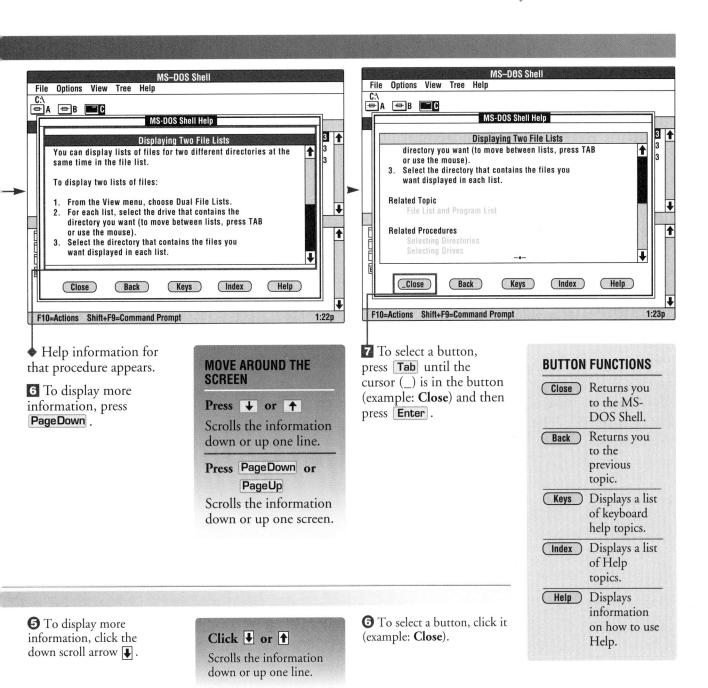

♦ Help information for that procedure appears.

6 To display more information, press **PageDown**.

MOVE AROUND THE SCREEN

Press ↓ or ↑
Scrolls the information down or up one line.

Press PageDown or PageUp
Scrolls the information down or up one screen.

7 To select a button, press **Tab** until the cursor (_) is in the button (example: **Close**) and then press **Enter**.

BUTTON FUNCTIONS

Close	Returns you to the MS-DOS Shell.
Back	Returns you to the previous topic.
Keys	Displays a list of keyboard help topics.
Index	Displays a list of Help topics.
Help	Displays information on how to use Help.

5 To display more information, click the down scroll arrow ↓.

Click ↓ or ↑
Scrolls the information down or up one line.

6 To select a button, click it (example: **Close**).

Change Drives

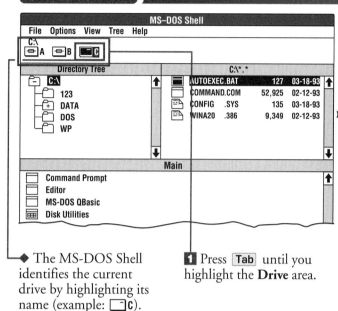

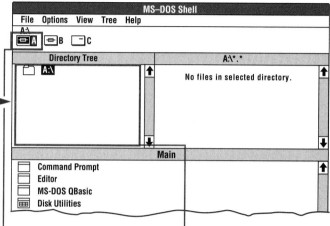

◆ The MS-DOS Shell identifies the current drive by highlighting its name (example: ☐C).

1 Press **Tab** until you highlight the **Drive** area.

2 Press **←** or **→** until you highlight the drive you want to change to (example: ☐A).

3 Press **Enter** and the **Directory Tree** area displays the directories in the new current drive.

Note: In this example, the diskette in drive A does not contain any files in the current directory.

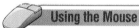

Using the Mouse

❶ To change to another drive, click its icon (example: ☐A).

Note: To change back to drive C, click ☐C.

Before changing to a floppy drive, make sure you insert a diskette into the drive.

Shortcut for Steps 1 to 3

To change to drive **A**, press **Ctrl** + **A**.

To change to drive **B**, press **Ctrl** + **B**.

To change to drive **C**, press **Ctrl** + **C**.

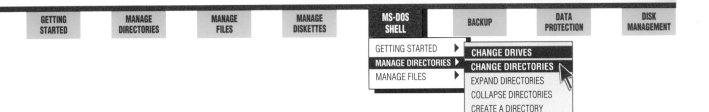

| GETTING STARTED | MANAGE DIRECTORIES | MANAGE FILES | MANAGE DISKETTES | MS-DOS SHELL | BACKUP | DATA PROTECTION | DISK MANAGEMENT |

GETTING STARTED ▶
MANAGE DIRECTORIES ▶ | CHANGE DRIVES
MANAGE FILES ▶ | CHANGE DIRECTORIES
EXPAND DIRECTORIES
COLLAPSE DIRECTORIES
CREATE A DIRECTORY

Change Directories

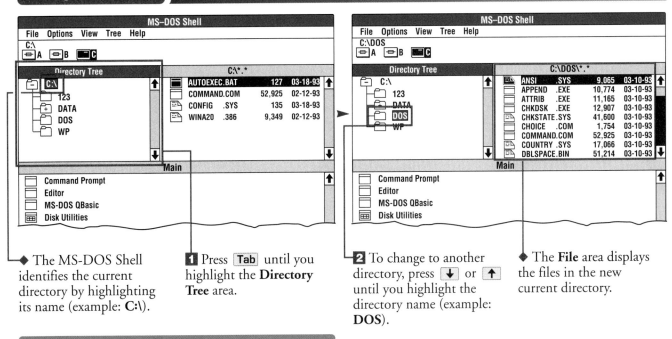

◆ The MS-DOS Shell identifies the current directory by highlighting its name (example: **C:**).

1 Press **Tab** until you highlight the **Directory Tree** area.

2 To change to another directory, press **↓** or **↑** until you highlight the directory name (example: **DOS**).

◆ The **File** area displays the files in the new current directory.

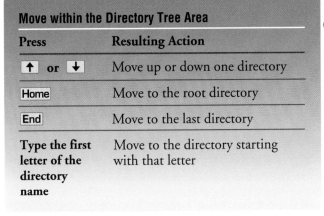

Move within the Directory Tree Area

Press	Resulting Action
↑ or **↓**	Move up or down one directory
Home	Move to the root directory
End	Move to the last directory
Type the first letter of the directory name	Move to the directory starting with that letter

Using the Mouse

① Click the name of the directory you want to change to (example: **DOS**).

67

Expand One Directory

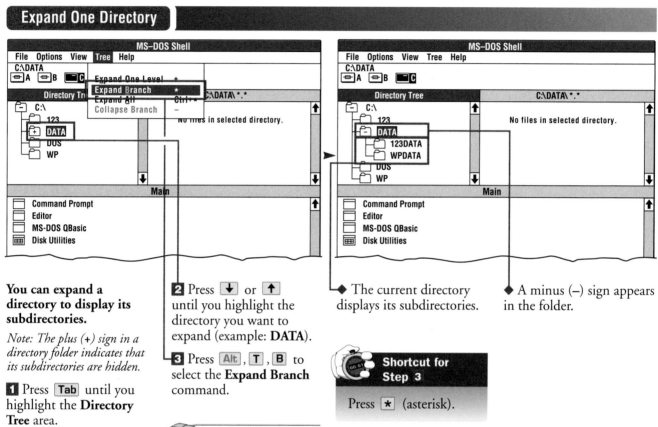

You can expand a directory to display its subdirectories.

Note: The plus (+) sign in a directory folder indicates that its subdirectories are hidden.

1 Press `Tab` until you highlight the **Directory Tree** area.

2 Press `↓` or `↑` until you highlight the directory you want to expand (example: **DATA**).

3 Press `Alt`, `T`, `B` to select the **Expand Branch** command.

Using the Mouse

❶ Click the name of the directory you want to expand (example: **DATA**).

❷ Click **Tree** to open its menu.

❸ Click **Expand Branch**.

◆ The current directory displays its subdirectories.

◆ A minus (–) sign appears in the folder.

Shortcut for Step 3

Press `*` (asterisk).

EXPAND ALL DIRECTORIES

1 Press `Tab` until you highlight the **Directory Tree** area.

2 Press `Alt`, `T`, `A` to select the **Expand All** command.

Using the Mouse

❶ Click **Tree** to open its menu.

❷ Click **Expand All**.

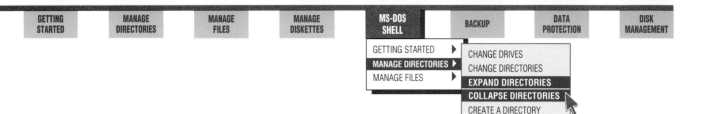

| GETTING STARTED | MANAGE DIRECTORIES | MANAGE FILES | MANAGE DISKETTES | MS-DOS SHELL | | BACKUP | DATA PROTECTION | DISK MANAGEMENT |

GETTING STARTED ▶
MANAGE DIRECTORIES ▶
MANAGE FILES ▶

CHANGE DRIVES
CHANGE DIRECTORIES
EXPAND DIRECTORIES
COLLAPSE DIRECTORIES
CREATE A DIRECTORY

Collapse One Directory

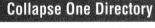

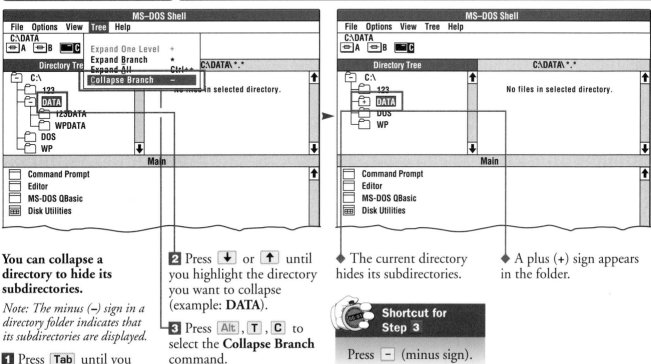

You can collapse a directory to hide its subdirectories.

Note: The minus (–) sign in a directory folder indicates that its subdirectories are displayed.

1 Press **Tab** until you highlight the **Directory Tree** area.

2 Press **↓** or **↑** until you highlight the directory you want to collapse (example: **DATA**).

3 Press **Alt**, **T**, **C** to select the **Collapse Branch** command.

Using the Mouse

① Click ⊟ beside the directory you want to collapse (example: **DATA**).

◆ The current directory hides its subdirectories.

◆ A plus (+) sign appears in the folder.

Shortcut for Step 3

Press **–** (minus sign).

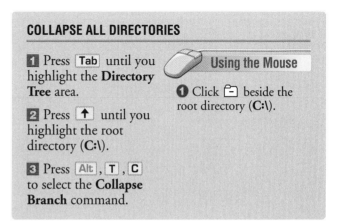

COLLAPSE ALL DIRECTORIES

1 Press **Tab** until you highlight the **Directory Tree** area.

2 Press **↑** until you highlight the root directory (**C:**).

3 Press **Alt**, **T**, **C** to select the **Collapse Branch** command.

Using the Mouse

① Click ⊟ beside the root directory (**C:**).

69

CREATE A DIRECTORY

Create a Directory

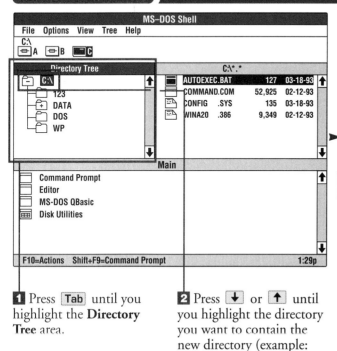

1 Press `Tab` until you highlight the **Directory Tree** area.

2 Press ↓ or ↑ until you highlight the directory you want to contain the new directory (example: **C:**).

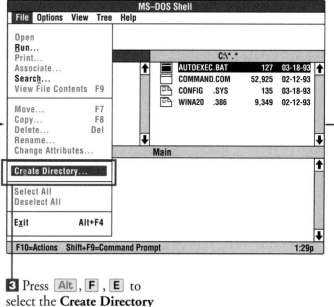

3 Press `Alt`, `F`, `E` to select the **Create Directory** command.

Directories help you organize the programs and data stored on your hard and floppy drives.

In this example, the GAMES directory is created one level below the root directory.

Using the Mouse

1 Click the directory you want to contain the new directory (example: **C:**).

2 Click **File** to open its menu.

3 Click **Create Directory**.

70

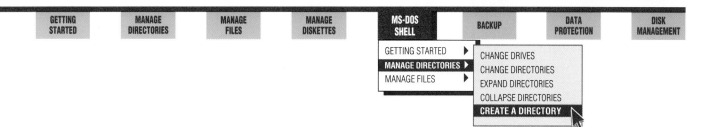

| GETTING STARTED | MANAGE DIRECTORIES | MANAGE FILES | MANAGE DISKETTES | MS-DOS SHELL | BACKUP | DATA PROTECTION | DISK MANAGEMENT |

GETTING STARTED ▶
MANAGE DIRECTORIES ▶
MANAGE FILES ▶

CHANGE DRIVES
CHANGE DIRECTORIES
EXPAND DIRECTORIES
COLLAPSE DIRECTORIES
CREATE A DIRECTORY

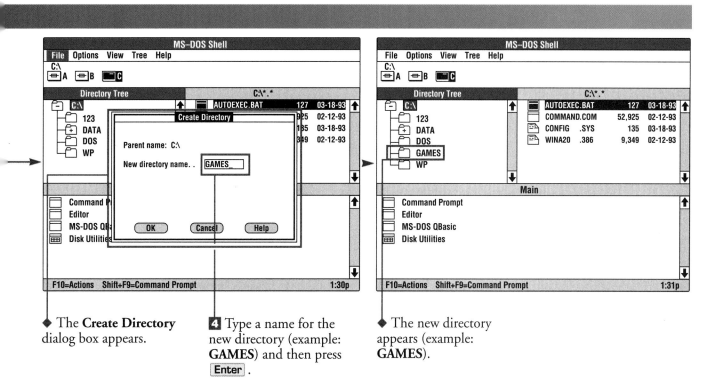

◆ The **Create Directory** dialog box appears.

4 Type a name for the new directory (example: **GAMES**) and then press **Enter**.

◆ The new directory appears (example: **GAMES**).

4 Type a name for the new directory (example: **GAMES**).

5 Click the **OK** button.

DELETE A DIRECTORY

1 Press **Tab** until you highlight the **Directory Tree** area.

2 Press **↓** or **↑** until you highlight the directory you want to delete.

3 Press **Alt**, **F**, **D** to select the **Delete** command.

4 Press **Enter**.

Using the Mouse

1 Click the directory you want to delete.

2 Click **File** to open its menu.

3 Click **Delete**.

4 Click the **Yes** button.

Note: You cannot delete a directory that contains subdirectories or files.

CHANGE VIEW

You can hide the Main area to increase the Directory Tree and File display areas.

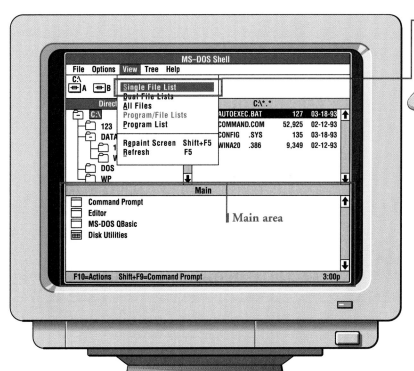

1 Press `Alt`, `V`, `S` to select the **Single File List** command.

Using the Mouse

1 Click **View** to open its menu.

2 Click **Single File List**.

GETTING STARTED ▶
MANAGE DIRECTORIES ▶
MANAGE FILES ▶ | CHANGE VIEW
SELECT FILES
SEARCH FOR FILES
SORT FILES
COPY FILES
RENAME A FILE
DELETE FILES

Single File List

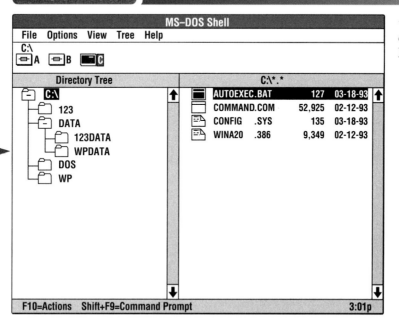

◆ The MS-DOS Shell changes to the **Single File List** view.

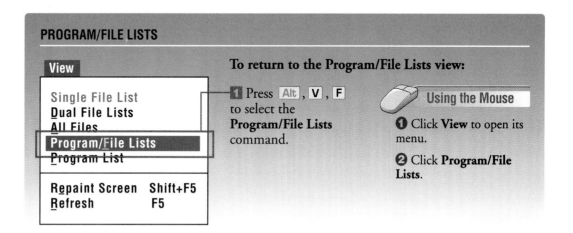

PROGRAM/FILE LISTS

View

Single File List
Dual File Lists
All Files
Program/File Lists
Program List

Repaint Screen   Shift+F5
Refresh   F5

To return to the Program/File Lists view:

1 Press `Alt`, `V`, `F` to select the **Program/File Lists** command.

Using the Mouse

1 Click **View** to open its menu.

2 Click **Program/File Lists**.

Select One File

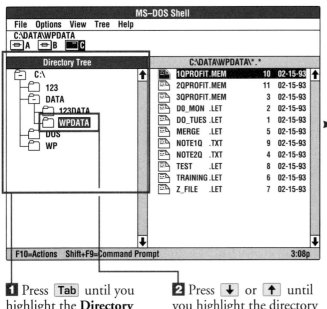

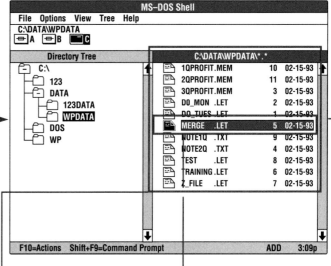

1 Press `Tab` until you highlight the **Directory Tree** area.

2 Press `↓` or `↑` until you highlight the directory that contains the file you want to select (example: **WPDATA**).

◆ The files in the highlighted directory appear.

3 Press `Tab` until you highlight the **File** area.

4 Press `↓` or `↑` until you highlight the file you want to select (example: **MERGE.LET**).

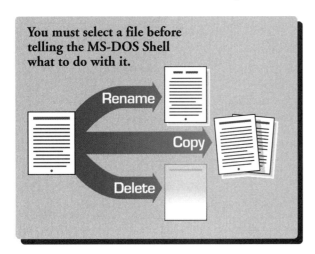

You must select a file before telling the MS-DOS Shell what to do with it.

Using the Mouse

1 Click the directory that contains the file you want to select (example: **WPDATA**).

2 Click the file you want to select (example: **MERGE.LET**).

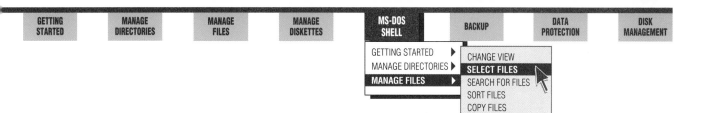

| GETTING STARTED | MANAGE DIRECTORIES | MANAGE FILES | MANAGE DISKETTES | MS–DOS SHELL | BACKUP | DATA PROTECTION | DISK MANAGEMENT |

GETTING STARTED ▶
MANAGE DIRECTORIES ▶
MANAGE FILES ▶

CHANGE VIEW
SELECT FILES
SEARCH FOR FILES
SORT FILES
COPY FILES
RENAME A FILE
DELETE FILES

Select Multiple Files

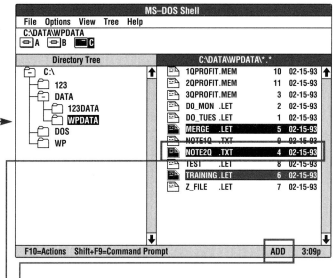

Select All Files

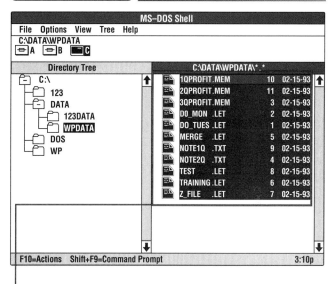

5 To select another file, press **Shift** + **F8** and the word **ADD** appears at the bottom of the screen.

6 Press ↓ or ↑ until you highlight the next file (example: **NOTE2Q.TXT**). Press the **Spacebar** to select it.

*Note: To deselect the file, press the **Spacebar** again.*

7 Repeat step **6** for each file you want to select.

8 Press **Shift** + **F8** to end the selection. The word **ADD** disappears.

1 Press **Alt**, **F**, **S** to select all files in the highlighted directory.

Shortcut

Press **Ctrl** + **/** (slash).

Using the Mouse

❶ Click **File** to open its menu.

❷ Click **Select All**.

❸ Hold down **Ctrl** as you click the other files you want to select.

DESELECT ALL FILES

1 To deselect all files, press ↓.

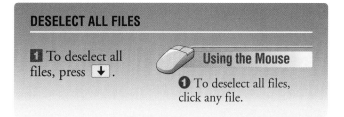

Using the Mouse

❶ To deselect all files, click any file.

SEARCH
FOR FILES

Search for Files

You can use
the MS-DOS
Shell to
search for a
file or group
of files.

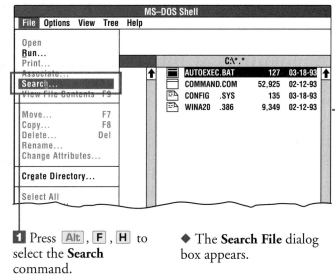

1 Press `Alt`, `F`, `H` to
select the **Search**
command.

◆ The **Search File** dialog
box appears.

 Using the Mouse

1 Click **File** to open its
menu.

2 Click **Search** and the
Search File dialog box
appears.

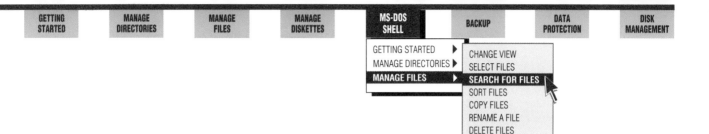

GETTING STARTED ▶
MANAGE DIRECTORIES ▶
MANAGE FILES ▶

CHANGE VIEW
SELECT FILES
SEARCH FOR FILES
SORT FILES
COPY FILES
RENAME A FILE
DELETE FILES

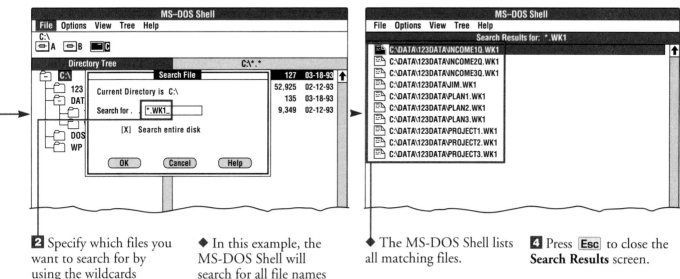

2 Specify which files you want to search for by using the wildcards (example: type *.**WK1**).

*Note: To search for a specific file, type its file name (example: **PLAN1.WK1**).*

◆ In this example, the MS-DOS Shell will search for all file names with the **WK1** extension.

3 Press **Enter** to start the search.

◆ The MS-DOS Shell lists all matching files.

4 Press **Esc** to close the **Search Results** screen.

You can move, copy, delete or rename the files listed in the **Search Results** screen.

3 Specify which files you want to search for by using the wildcards (example: type *.**WK1**).

*Note: To search for a specific file, type its file name (example: **PLAN1.WK1**).*

4 Click the **OK** button to start the search.

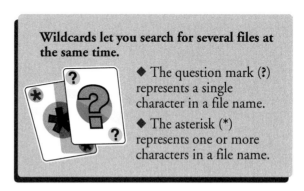

Wildcards let you search for several files at the same time.

◆ The question mark (**?**) represents a single character in a file name.

◆ The asterisk (*) represents one or more characters in a file name.

Sort Files

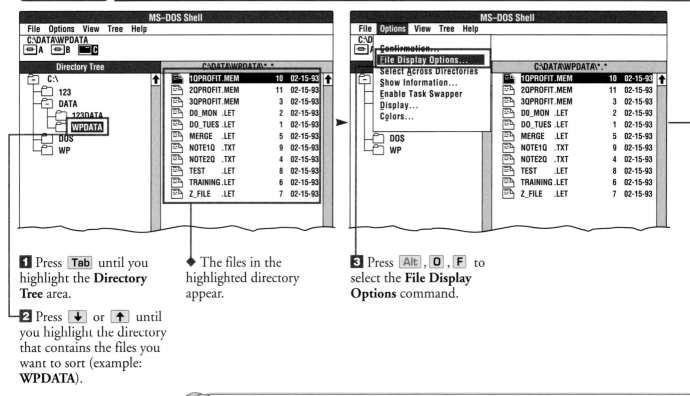

1 Press `Tab` until you highlight the **Directory Tree** area.

2 Press `↓` or `↑` until you highlight the directory that contains the files you want to sort (example: **WPDATA**).

◆ The files in the highlighted directory appear.

3 Press `Alt`, `O`, `F` to select the **File Display Options** command.

Using the Mouse

❶ Click the directory that contains the files you want to sort (example: **WPDATA**).

❷ Click **Options** to open its menu.

❸ Click **File Display Options** and its dialog box appears.

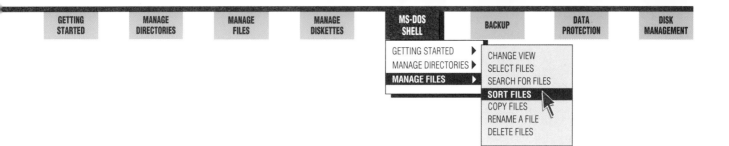

GETTING STARTED ▶
MANAGE DIRECTORIES ▶
MANAGE FILES ▶

CHANGE VIEW
SELECT FILES
SEARCH FOR FILES
SORT FILES
COPY FILES
RENAME A FILE
DELETE FILES

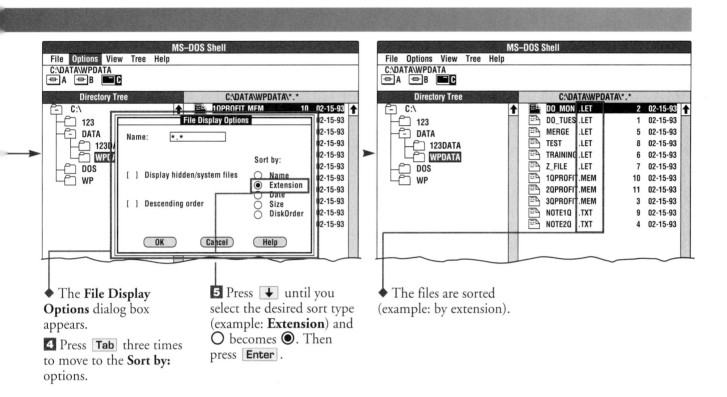

◆ The **File Display Options** dialog box appears.

4 Press `Tab` three times to move to the **Sort by:** options.

5 Press `↓` until you select the desired sort type (example: **Extension**) and ○ becomes ●. Then press `Enter`.

◆ The files are sorted (example: by extension).

4 Click the circle beside the desired sort type (example: **Extension**) and ○ becomes ●.

5 Click the **OK** button.

You can sort files by name, extension, date or size.

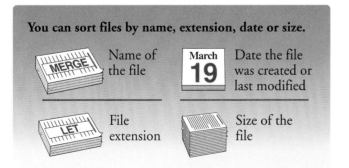

Name of the file

Date the file was created or last modified

File extension

Size of the file

COPY FILES

The MS-DOS Shell lets you make an exact copy of a file and place it in a new location. The original file remains unaffected.

In this example, the TRAINING.LET file is copied to a diskette in drive A.

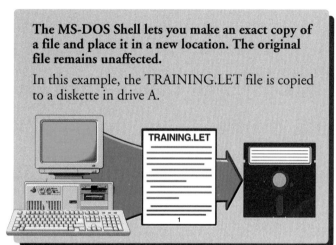

Note: Before copying files to a floppy drive, make sure you insert a diskette into the drive.

Copy Files

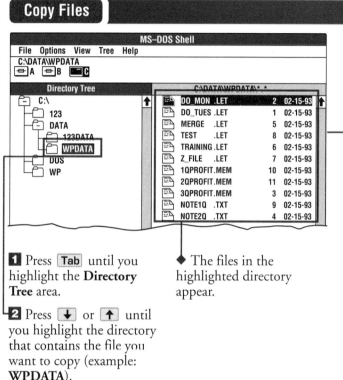

1 Press `Tab` until you highlight the **Directory Tree** area.

2 Press ↓ or ↑ until you highlight the directory that contains the file you want to copy (example: **WPDATA**).

◆ The files in the highlighted directory appear.

Using the Mouse

1 Click the directory that contains the file you want to copy (example: **WPDATA**).

2 Click the file you want to copy (example: **TRAINING.LET**).

*Note: To copy more than one file, select them in step **2**. To select multiple files, refer to page 74.*

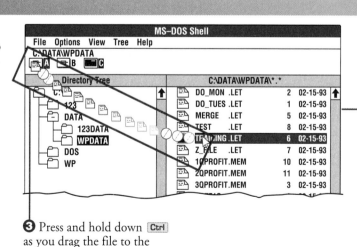

3 Press and hold down `Ctrl` as you drag the file to the drive (▭) or directory (🗀) you want to copy it to.

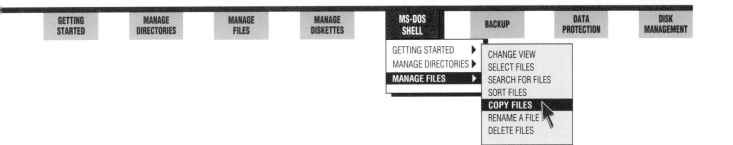

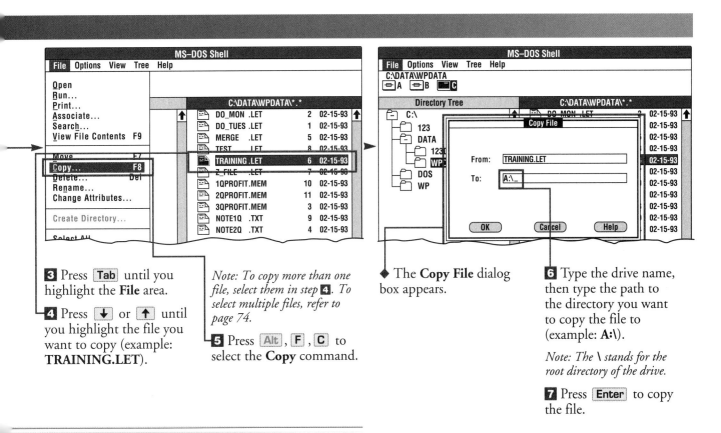

3 Press `Tab` until you highlight the **File** area.

4 Press `↓` or `↑` until you highlight the file you want to copy (example: **TRAINING.LET**).

Note: To copy more than one file, select them in step **4**. *To select multiple files, refer to page 74.*

5 Press `Alt`, `F`, `C` to select the **Copy** command.

◆ The **Copy File** dialog box appears.

6 Type the drive name, then type the path to the directory you want to copy the file to (example: **A:**).

Note: The \\ stands for the root directory of the drive.

7 Press `Enter` to copy the file.

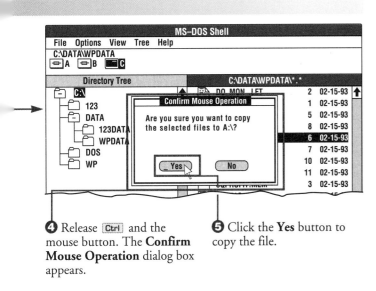

4 Release `Ctrl` and the mouse button. The **Confirm Mouse Operation** dialog box appears.

5 Click the **Yes** button to copy the file.

RENAME A FILE

Rename a File

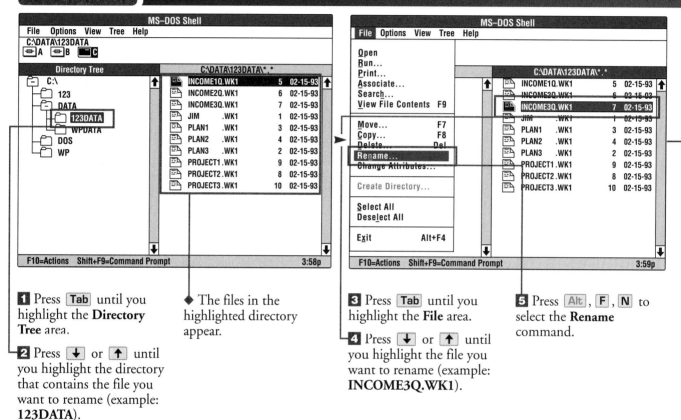

1 Press `Tab` until you highlight the **Directory Tree** area.

2 Press `↓` or `↑` until you highlight the directory that contains the file you want to rename (example: **123DATA**).

◆ The files in the highlighted directory appear.

3 Press `Tab` until you highlight the **File** area.

4 Press `↓` or `↑` until you highlight the file you want to rename (example: **INCOME3Q.WK1**).

5 Press `Alt`, `F`, `N` to select the **Rename** command.

Using the Mouse

❶ Click the directory that contains the file you want to rename (example: **123DATA**).

❷ Click the file you want to rename (example: **INCOME3Q.WK1**).

❸ Click **File** to open its menu.

❹ Click **Rename** and the **Rename File** dialog box appears.

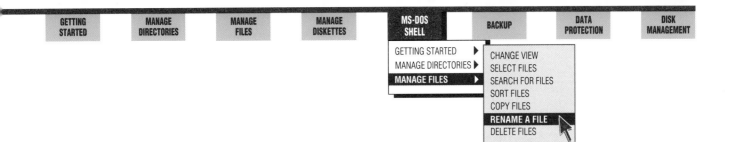

GETTING STARTED ▶
MANAGE DIRECTORIES ▶
MANAGE FILES ▶

CHANGE VIEW
SELECT FILES
SEARCH FOR FILES
SORT FILES
COPY FILES
RENAME A FILE
DELETE FILES

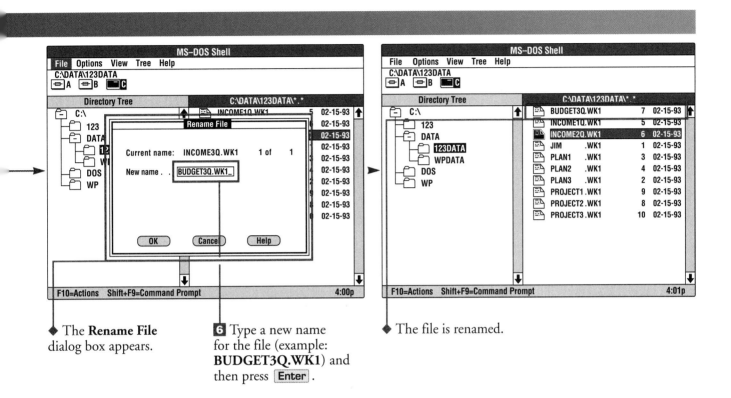

◆ The **Rename File** dialog box appears.

6 Type a new name for the file (example: **BUDGET3Q.WK1**) and then press Enter.

◆ The file is renamed.

5 Type a new name for the file (example: **BUDGET3Q.WK1**).

6 Click the **OK** button.

In this example, the INCOME3Q.WK1 file was renamed BUDGET3Q.WK1.

Delete Files

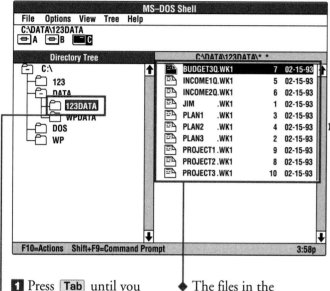

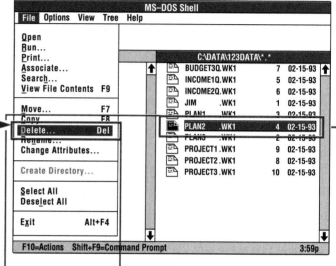

1 Press `Tab` until you highlight the **Directory Tree** area.

2 Press `↓` or `↑` until you highlight the directory that contains the file you want to delete (example: **123DATA**).

♦ The files in the highlighted directory appear.

3 Press `Tab` until you highlight the **File** area.

4 Press `↓` or `↑` until you highlight the file you want to delete (example: **PLAN2.WK1**).

Note: To delete more than one file, select them in step **4**. *To select multiple files, refer to page 74.*

5 Press `Alt`, `F`, `D` to select the **Delete** command.

Using the Mouse

1 Click the directory that contains the file you want to delete (example: **123DATA**).

2 Click the file you want to delete (example: **PLAN2.WK1**).

Note: To delete more than one file, select them in step **2**. *To select multiple files, refer to page 74.*

3 Click **File** to open its menu.

4 Click **Delete** and the **Delete File Confirmation** dialog box appears.

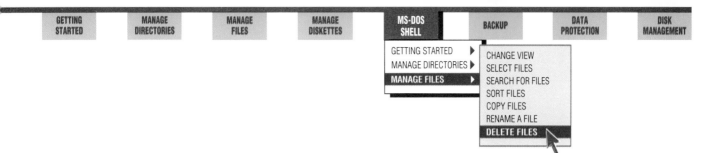

GETTING STARTED	MANAGE DIRECTORIES	MANAGE FILES	MANAGE DISKETTES	MS-DOS SHELL	BACKUP	DATA PROTECTION	DISK MANAGEMENT

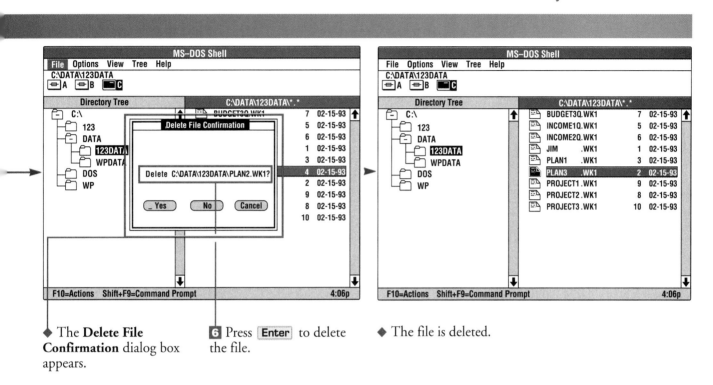

◆ The **Delete File Confirmation** dialog box appears.

6 Press **Enter** to delete the file.

◆ The file is deleted.

5 Click the **Yes** button to delete the file.

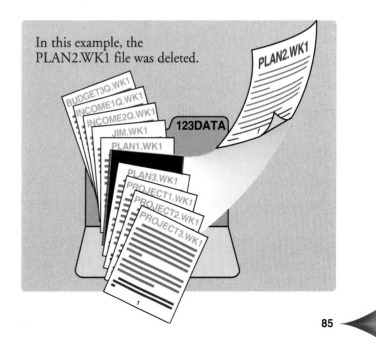

In this example, the PLAN2.WK1 file was deleted.

Why Use Microsoft Backup?

PROTECT DATA

You can use Microsoft Backup to copy your files onto diskettes or other media. This way, you can replace lost data if your hard drive fails or you accidentally erase important files.

FREE UP HARD DISK SPACE

You can use Microsoft Backup to copy old or less-used files onto diskettes or other media. You can then remove these files from your hard drive to free disk space.

TRANSFER FILES TO ANOTHER COMPUTER

You can use Microsoft Backup to move your files to another computer.

INTRODUCTION
BACKUP SCHEDULE
START BACKUP
BACK UP YOUR FILES
RESTORE YOUR FILES

Backup Media

Most of your program and data files are stored on your hard drive. You can use Microsoft Backup to copy these files to the following media:

DISKETTES

Diskettes are ideal for small backups (files totaling less than 20 megabytes).

NETWORK DRIVES

Network drives offer a secure environment for your backups. Ask your Network Administrator how to back up your files on a network.

OTHER MEDIA

Optical drives, removable hard disk cartridges and Bernoulli drives are practical for large backups (files totaling 20 megabytes or more).

Backup Schedule

Back up your work frequently. Ask yourself, "How much work can I afford to lose?" If it is only a day's worth, then make daily backups.

If your files do not often change during the week, back up weekly.

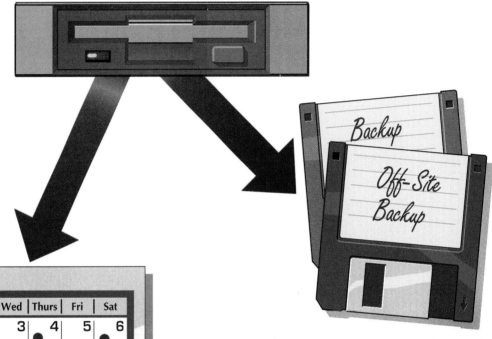

◆ Minimize your chances of losing important data by making at least two sets of backups.

Keep one set near your computer and the other set "off-site" in a safety-deposit box or in another building.

◆ Make a backup schedule and stick to it! Hard drive disasters always seem to happen right after you miss a scheduled backup.

| GETTING STARTED | MANAGE DIRECTORIES | MANAGE FILES | MANAGE DISKETTES | MS-DOS SHELL | BACKUP | DATA PROTECTION | DISK MANAGEMENT |

INTRODUCTION
BACKUP SCHEDULE
START BACKUP
BACK UP YOUR FILES
RESTORE YOUR FILES

Start Microsoft Backup

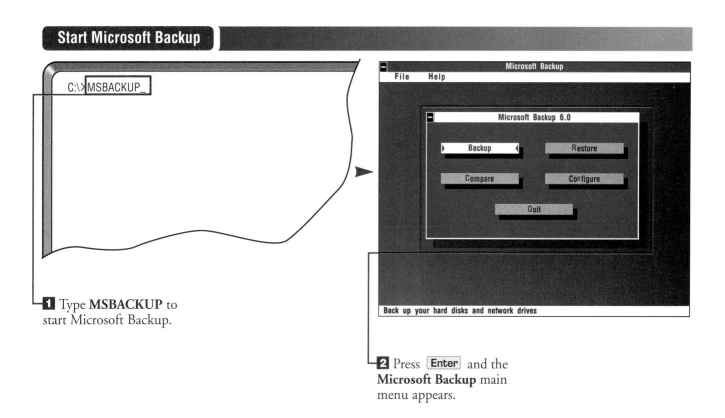

C:\>MSBACKUP_

1 Type **MSBACKUP** to start Microsoft Backup.

2 Press **Enter** and the **Microsoft Backup** main menu appears.

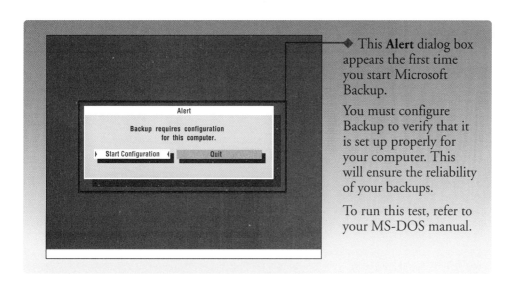

◆ This **Alert** dialog box appears the first time you start Microsoft Backup.

You must configure Backup to verify that it is set up properly for your computer. This will ensure the reliability of your backups.

To run this test, refer to your MS-DOS manual.

BACK UP
YOUR FILES

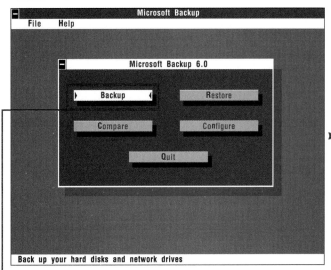

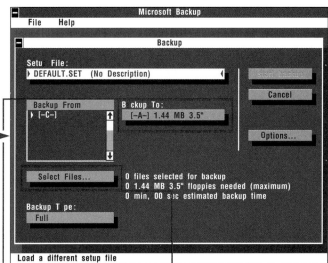

1 Type **B** (for **B**ackup) and the **Backup** dialog box appears.

◆ The **Backup To:** box displays the size and type of diskette you will copy your files to.

*Note: To choose a different diskette, refer to **Change Backup Destination** below.*

2 Type **L** (for Select Files) and the **Select Backup Files** dialog box appears.

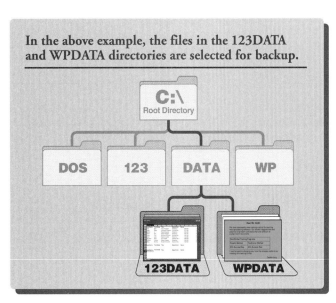

In the above example, the files in the 123DATA and WPDATA directories are selected for backup.

CHANGE BACKUP DESTINATION

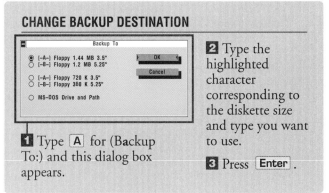

1 Type **A** for (Backup To:) and this dialog box appears.

2 Type the highlighted character corresponding to the diskette size and type you want to use.

3 Press **Enter**.

| GETTING STARTED | MANAGE DIRECTORIES | MANAGE FILES | MANAGE DISKETTES | MS-DOS SHELL | BACKUP | DATA PROTECTION | DISK MANAGEMENT |

INTRODUCTION
BACKUP SCHEDULE
START BACKUP
BACK UP YOUR FILES
RESTORE YOUR FILES

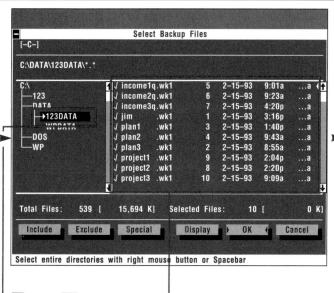

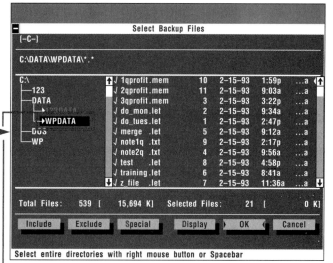

3 Press ↓ until you highlight the directory containing the files you want to back up (example: **123DATA**).

◆ This area displays the files in the highlighted directory.

4 Press the **Spacebar** to select all the files in that directory. The files now display a check mark (✓) beside their names.

*Note: To deselect the files, press the **Spacebar** again.*

◆ To back up files in additional directories, repeat steps **3** and **4**.

◆ In this example, the files in the **WPDATA** directory are also selected for backup.

5 Press **Enter** to return to the **Backup** dialog box.

Microsoft Backup remembers the last files you backed up. The next time you want to back up the same data, you can eliminate steps **2** through **5**.

91

BACK UP
YOUR FILES

Step 2: Start the Backup

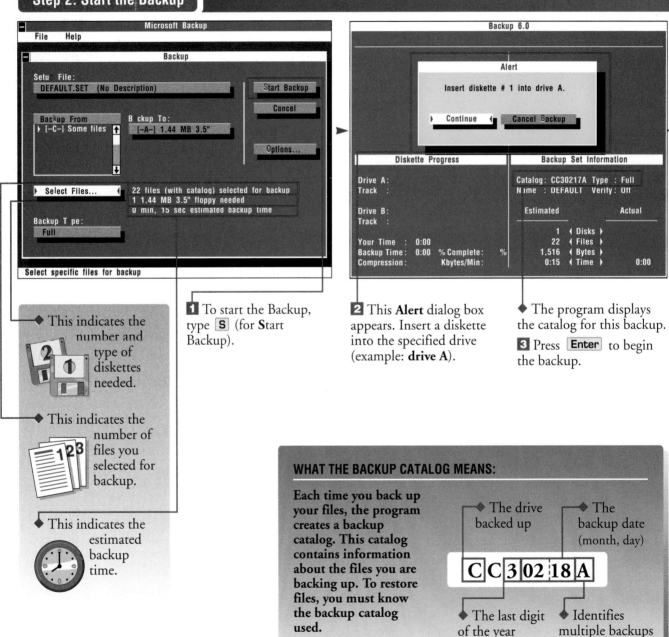

1 To start the Backup, type **S** (for **S**tart Backup).

♦ This indicates the number and type of diskettes needed.

♦ This indicates the number of files you selected for backup.

♦ This indicates the estimated backup time.

2 This **Alert** dialog box appears. Insert a diskette into the specified drive (example: **drive A**).

♦ The program displays the catalog for this backup.

3 Press **Enter** to begin the backup.

WHAT THE BACKUP CATALOG MEANS:

Each time you back up your files, the program creates a backup catalog. This catalog contains information about the files you are backing up. To restore files, you must know the backup catalog used.

♦ The drive backed up

♦ The backup date (month, day)

C C 3 02 18 A

♦ The last digit of the year

♦ Identifies multiple backups on the same day

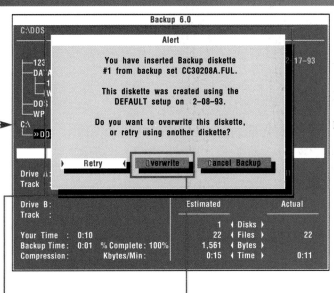

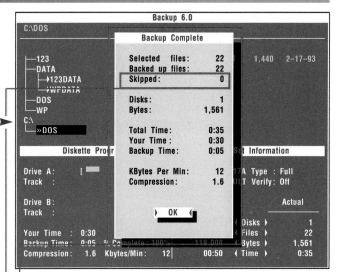

◆ This **Alert** dialog box appears if you have inserted a diskette used for another backup.

4 To overwrite (replace) the files, type **O** (for **O**verwrite).

Note: To retain the files, use a new diskette.

5 If you require more than one diskette, follow the screen prompts for inserting them.

◆ The **Backup Complete** dialog box appears when the backup is complete.

◆ Check to ensure no files were skipped.

6 Press **Enter** to return to the **Microsoft Backup** main menu.

7 To return to the command prompt, type **Q** (for **Q**uit).

◆ Write the backup catalog on your diskette. If you use more than one diskette, number them sequentially.

RESTORE YOUR FILES

You can restore lost data if your hard drive fails or you accidentally erase important information. The Restore feature copies the files from your backup diskettes to your hard drive.

Step 1: Select Catalog

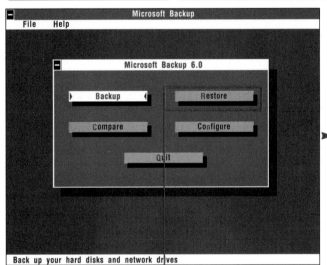

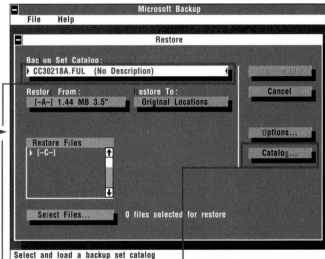

You must tell Microsoft Backup which catalog identifies the files you want to restore.

1 To start Microsoft Backup from the command prompt, type **MSBACKUP** and then press `Enter`.

2 Type `R` (for **R**estore) and the **Restore** dialog box appears.

◆ Microsoft Backup displays the catalog that identifies the files it will restore.

3 To restore a different catalog, type `G` (for Catalo**g**) and the **Select Catalog** dialog box appears.

INTRODUCTION
BACKUP SCHEDULE
START BACKUP
BACK UP YOUR FILES
RESTORE YOUR FILES

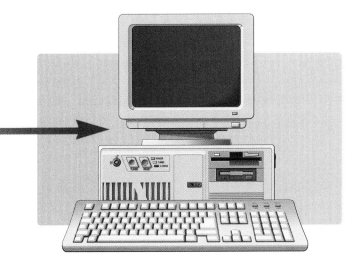

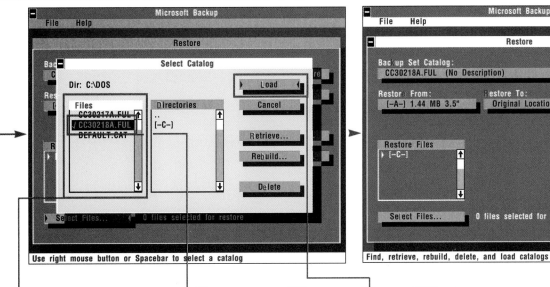

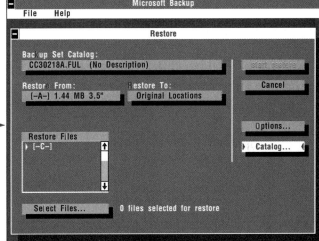

Use right mouse button or Spacebar to select a catalog

Find, retrieve, rebuild, delete, and load catalogs

◆ The **Files** box displays the catalog names for all your backups. The catalog name identifying your last backup displays a check mark (✓) beside it.

4 Press ↓ or ↑ until you highlight the catalog that identifies the files you want to restore.

5 Press the **Spacebar** to select the catalog. A check mark (✓) appears beside it.

6 Press **Tab** twice to select **Load** and then press **Enter**.

◆ You are returned to the **Restore** dialog box.

◆ To restore your files, refer to the next page.

95

RESTORE
YOUR FILES

Step 2: Select Files

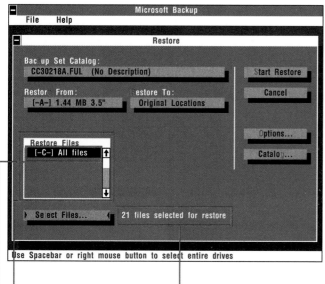

Use Spacebar or right mouse button to select entire drives

1 Type **I** (for Restore Files) to select the **Restore Files** box.

2 Press the **Spacebar** to restore all files on the drive.

◆ Microsoft Backup indicates the number of files selected for restore.

Note: Backup created an extra file to store the catalog information.

Step 3: Start Restore

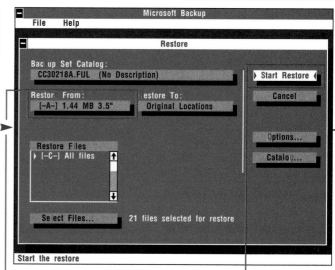

Start the restore

◆ The **Restore From:** box displays the size and type of diskette you will restore your files from.

*Note: To choose a different diskette, refer to **Change Restore Source** below.*

3 Press **Tab** until you select **Start Restore** and then press **Enter**.

Before restoring your files, make sure you are ready to insert the diskettes. Check to ensure the diskettes contain the files you want to restore.

CHANGE RESTORE SOURCE

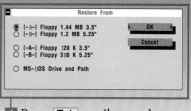

1 Press **Tab** until you select **Restore From:** and then press **Enter**. This dialog box appears.

2 Type the highlighted character corresponding to the diskette size and type you want to use.

3 Press **Enter**.

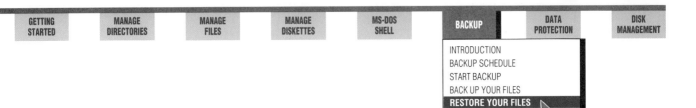

| GETTING STARTED | MANAGE DIRECTORIES | MANAGE FILES | MANAGE DISKETTES | MS-DOS SHELL | BACKUP | DATA PROTECTION | DISK MANAGEMENT |

INTRODUCTION
BACKUP SCHEDULE
START BACKUP
BACK UP YOUR FILES
RESTORE YOUR FILES

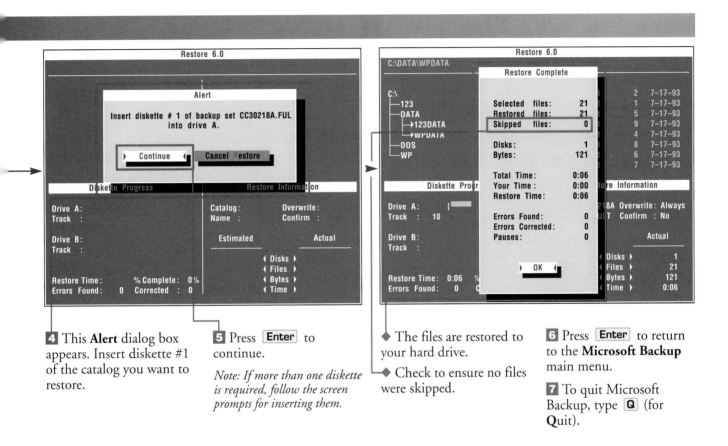

4 This **Alert** dialog box appears. Insert diskette #1 of the catalog you want to restore.

5 Press **Enter** to continue.

Note: If more than one diskette is required, follow the screen prompts for inserting them.

◆ The files are restored to your hard drive.

◆ Check to ensure no files were skipped.

6 Press **Enter** to return to the **Microsoft Backup** main menu.

7 To quit Microsoft Backup, type **Q** (for **Quit**).

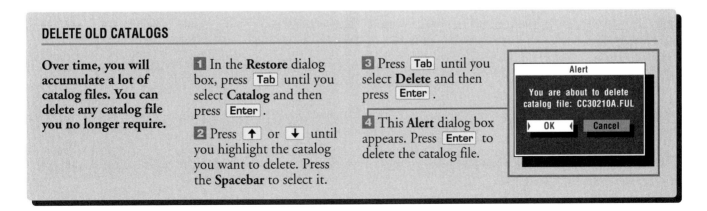

DELETE OLD CATALOGS

Over time, you will accumulate a lot of catalog files. You can delete any catalog file you no longer require.

1 In the **Restore** dialog box, press **Tab** until you select **Catalog** and then press **Enter**.

2 Press ↑ or ↓ until you highlight the catalog you want to delete. Press the **Spacebar** to select it.

3 Press **Tab** until you select **Delete** and then press **Enter**.

4 This **Alert** dialog box appears. Press **Enter** to delete the catalog file.

97

DELETE SENTRY

Delete Sentry protects your data from permanent loss. Use it to restore files you have accidentally deleted.

Here's how it works...

◆ Delete Sentry is a small program you load into your computer's electronic memory. It watches for files being deleted.

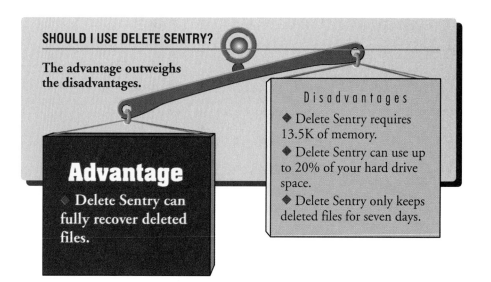

SHOULD I USE DELETE SENTRY?

The advantage outweighs the disadvantages.

Advantage
◆ Delete Sentry can fully recover deleted files.

Disadvantages
◆ Delete Sentry requires 13.5K of memory.

◆ Delete Sentry can use up to 20% of your hard drive space.

◆ Delete Sentry only keeps deleted files for seven days.

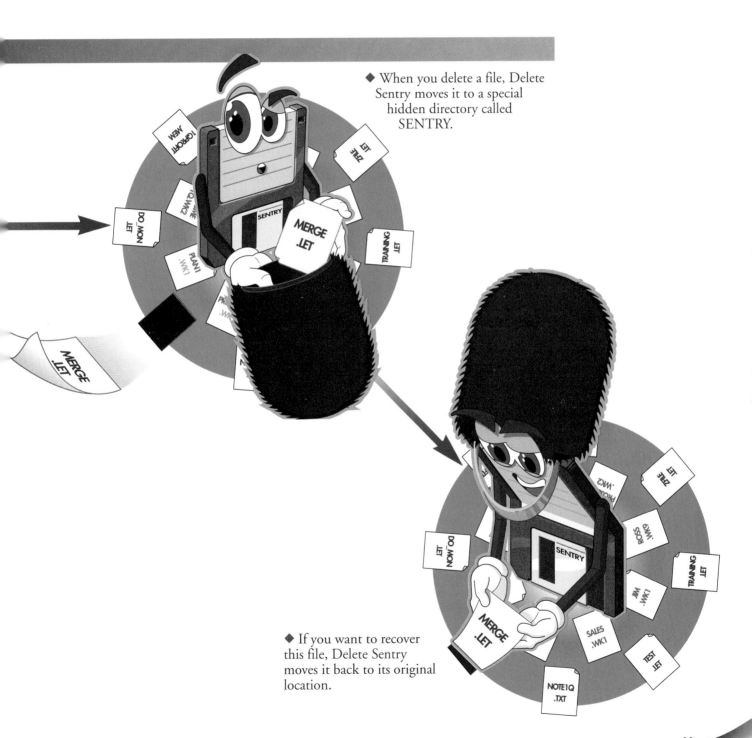

◆ When you delete a file, Delete Sentry moves it to a special hidden directory called SENTRY.

◆ If you want to recover this file, Delete Sentry moves it back to its original location.

DELETE SENTRY

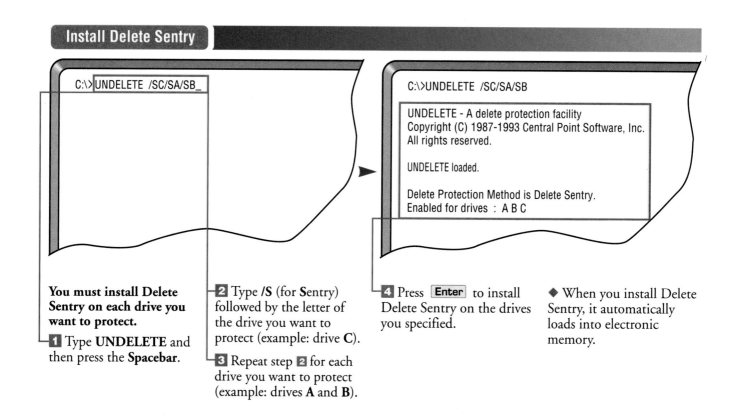

```
C:\>UNDELETE /SC/SA/SB_
```

```
C:\>UNDELETE /SC/SA/SB

UNDELETE - A delete protection facility
Copyright (C) 1987-1993 Central Point Software, Inc.
All rights reserved.

UNDELETE loaded.

Delete Protection Method is Delete Sentry.
Enabled for drives : A B C
```

You must install Delete Sentry on each drive you want to protect.

1 Type **UNDELETE** and then press the **Spacebar**.

2 Type **/S** (for **S**entry) followed by the letter of the drive you want to protect (example: drive **C**).

3 Repeat step **2** for each drive you want to protect (example: drives **A** and **B**).

4 Press **Enter** to install Delete Sentry on the drives you specified.

◆ When you install Delete Sentry, it automatically loads into electronic memory.

IMPORTANT!

You only need to **install** Delete Sentry once. However, you must **load** Delete Sentry each time you turn on your computer.

DELETE SENTRY
ANTI-VIRUS

Load Delete Sentry

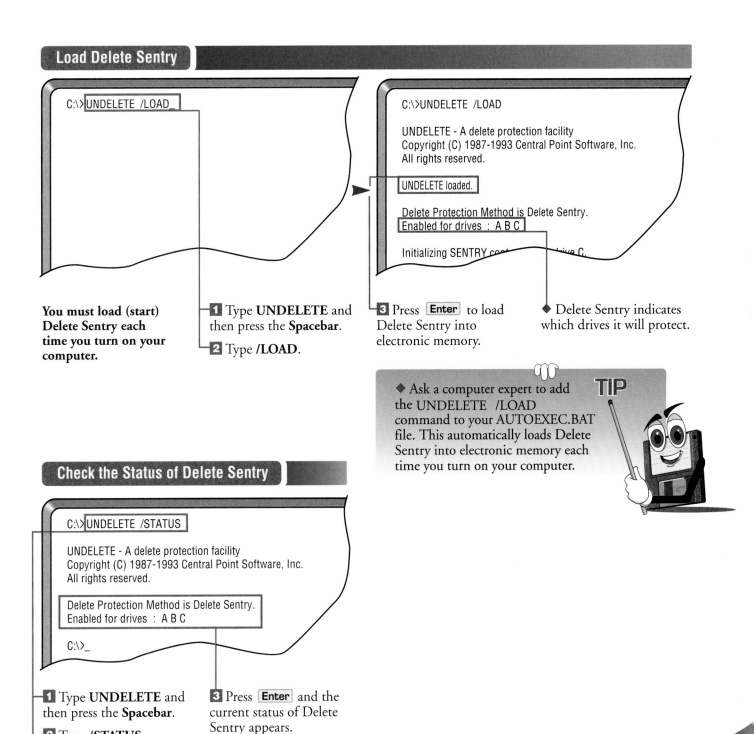

C:\>UNDELETE /LOAD_

C:\>UNDELETE /LOAD

UNDELETE - A delete protection facility
Copyright (C) 1987-1993 Central Point Software, Inc.
All rights reserved.

UNDELETE loaded.

Delete Protection Method is Delete Sentry.
Enabled for drives : A B C

Initializing SENTRY con................. rive C.

You must load (start) Delete Sentry each time you turn on your computer.

1 Type **UNDELETE** and then press the **Spacebar**.

2 Type **/LOAD**.

3 Press **Enter** to load Delete Sentry into electronic memory.

◆ Delete Sentry indicates which drives it will protect.

◆ Ask a computer expert to add the UNDELETE /LOAD command to your AUTOEXEC.BAT file. This automatically loads Delete Sentry into electronic memory each time you turn on your computer.

TIP

Check the Status of Delete Sentry

C:\>UNDELETE /STATUS

UNDELETE - A delete protection facility
Copyright (C) 1987-1993 Central Point Software, Inc.
All rights reserved.

Delete Protection Method is Delete Sentry.
Enabled for drives : A B C

C:\>_

1 Type **UNDELETE** and then press the **Spacebar**.

2 Type **/STATUS**.

3 Press **Enter** and the current status of Delete Sentry appears.

DELETE SENTRY

```
C:\DATA\123DATA>DEL PLAN2.WK1

C:\DATA\123DATA>_
```

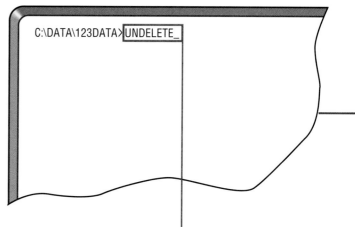

```
C:\DATA\123DATA>UNDELETE_
```

Before using the Delete command, make sure you load the Delete Sentry program.

1 Change to the directory that contains the file you want to delete.

Note: For example, to change to the \DATA\123DATA directory, type CD \DATA\123DATA and then press Enter*.*

2 Type **DEL** and then press the **Spacebar**.

3 Type the name of the file you want to delete (example: **PLAN2.WK1**) and then press Enter .

◆ Delete Sentry moves the file to a special hidden directory.

1 Change to the directory that originally contained the deleted files.

2 Type **UNDELETE** and then press Enter .

RECOVER ONE FILE

Use this method if you know the name of the file you want to recover.

1 Type **UNDELETE** and then press the **Spacebar**.

2 Type the name of the file you want to recover (example: **PLAN2.WK1**) and then press Enter .

3 Type Y (for **Y**es) to recover the file.

RECOVER ALL FILES AT THE SAME TIME

1 Type **UNDELETE** and then press the **Spacebar**.

2 Type **/ALL** and then press Enter .

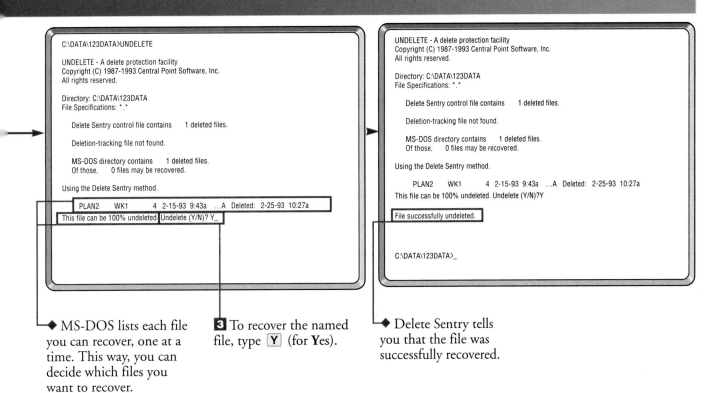

```
C:\DATA\123DATA>UNDELETE

UNDELETE - A delete protection facility
Copyright (C) 1987-1993 Central Point Software, Inc.
All rights reserved.

Directory: C:\DATA\123DATA
File Specifications: *.*

    Delete Sentry control file contains      1 deleted files.

    Deletion-tracking file not found.

    MS-DOS directory contains      1 deleted files.
    Of those,      0 files may be recovered.

Using the Delete Sentry method.

      PLAN2      WK1        4  2-15-93  9:43a   ...A  Deleted:  2-25-93  10:27a
This file can be 100% undeleted  Undelete (Y/N)? Y_
```

```
UNDELETE - A delete protection facility
Copyright (C) 1987-1993 Central Point Software, Inc.
All rights reserved.

Directory: C:\DATA\123DATA
File Specifications: *.*

    Delete Sentry control file contains      1 deleted files.

    Deletion-tracking file not found.

    MS-DOS directory contains      1 deleted files.
    Of those,      0 files may be recovered.

Using the Delete Sentry method.

      PLAN2      WK1        4  2-15-93  9:43a   ...A  Deleted:  2-25-93  10:27a
This file can be 100% undeleted. Undelete (Y/N)?Y

File successfully undeleted.


C:\DATA\123DATA>_
```

◆ MS-DOS lists each file you can recover, one at a time. This way, you can decide which files you want to recover.

Note: Delete Sentry only keeps your deleted files for seven days. To lengthen or shorten this time period, ask a computer expert.

3 To recover the named file, type **Y** (for **Y**es).

◆ Delete Sentry tells you that the file was successfully recovered.

TIP To free disk space, you can purge (permanently erase) all the files stored in Delete Sentry's hidden directory. Do this only after recovering all the files you need.

1 Type **UNDELETE** and then press the **Spacebar**.

2 Type **/PURGE** and then press **Enter**.

Note: This purges the files on the current drive.

ANTI-VIRUS

Computer viruses are programs that multiply and spread to many computers without being detected.

Eventually, most viruses reveal their presence by displaying messages on the screen or by damaging files or entire hard drives.

MS-DOS includes two programs to protect your computer from viruses. They are: **MSAV** (Microsoft **A**nti-**V**irus) and **VSafe** (**V**irus **Safe**).

The VSafe and MSAV Partnership

Use both VSafe and MSAV for maximum protection against viruses.

◆ VSafe *continuously* checks for viruses and alerts you if it detects one. VSafe cannot destroy a virus. To remove a virus from your computer, use MSAV.

◆ MSAV detects and destroys viruses, but only when you instruct it to do so.

Note: New viruses are created every day. To protect your computer, periodically update your VSafe and MSAV programs. Consult your MS-DOS manual for more details.

| GETTING STARTED | MANAGE DIRECTORIES | MANAGE FILES | MANAGE DISKETTES | MS-DOS SHELL | BACKUP | DATA PROTECTION | DISK MANAGEMENT |

DELETE SENTRY
ANTI-VIRUS

How Viruses Infect Your Computer

DISKETTES

Viruses can hide inside programs stored on diskettes. They can also exist on diskettes that do not contain files. Four of the five most common viruses in the United States are spread by starting a computer with an infected diskette in a floppy drive.

MODEMS

Modems allow computers to transfer information over telephone lines. Viruses can attach themselves to the data being transferred and infect your computer. BBS's (Bulletin Board Systems) are particularly vulnerable.

NETWORKS

Networks link computers together to share data and programs. Viruses can quickly spread through a network. To protect your computer, ask your network administrator for virus protection information.

ANTI-VIRUS

Start VSafe

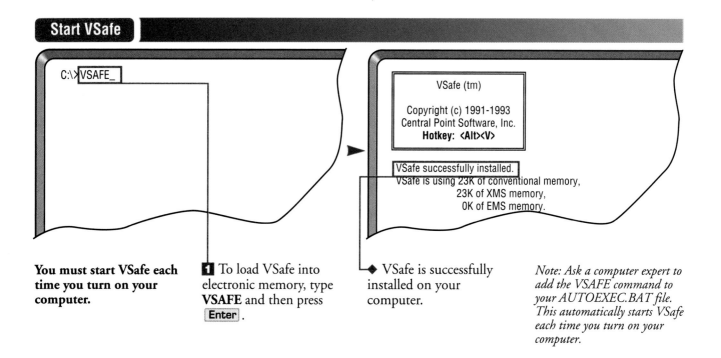

```
C:\>VSAFE_
```

```
          VSafe (tm)

     Copyright (c) 1991-1993
    Central Point Software, Inc.
      Hotkey:  <Alt><V>
```

```
VSafe successfully installed.
```
VSafe is using 23K of conventional memory,
23K of XMS memory,
0K of EMS memory.

You must start VSafe each time you turn on your computer.

1 To load VSafe into electronic memory, type **VSAFE** and then press `Enter`.

◆ VSafe is successfully installed on your computer.

Note: Ask a computer expert to add the VSAFE command to your AUTOEXEC.BAT file. This automatically starts VSafe each time you turn on your computer.

Virus Protection Plan

◆ Start VSafe immediately after turning on your computer.

◆ Use MSAV to check all new diskettes.

◆ Never start your computer with a diskette in a drive. If you accidentally do so, immediately use MSAV to check your computer.

◆ Use MSAV to check your hard drive at least once a month.

◆ If someone else uses your computer, use MSAV to check for viruses. This includes repair shops, friends and co-workers.

◆ Use MSAV to check your hard drive after receiving files through a modem.

DELETE SENTRY
ANTI-VIRUS

Start MSAV

C:\>MSAV_

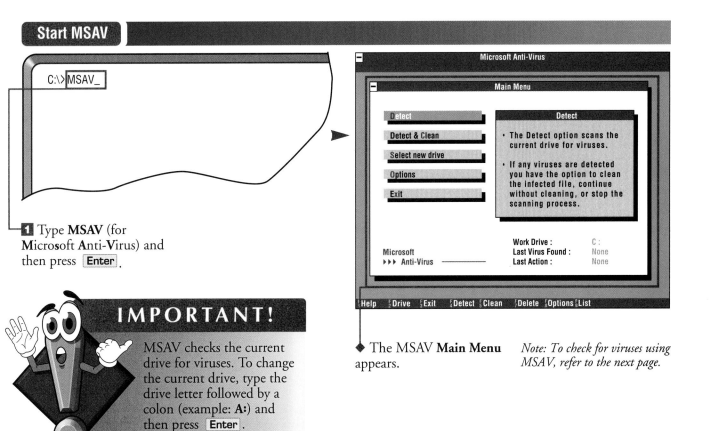

Microsoft Anti-Virus

Main Menu

Detect
Detect & Clean
Select new drive
Options
Exit

Detect

- The Detect option scans the current drive for viruses.

- If any viruses are detected you have the option to clean the infected file, continue without cleaning, or stop the scanning process.

Microsoft
▶▶▶ Anti-Virus ──────

Work Drive :   C :
Last Virus Found :   None
Last Action :   None

Help Drive Exit Detect Clean Delete Options List

1 Type **MSAV** (for Microsoft Anti-Virus) and then press **Enter**.

IMPORTANT!

MSAV checks the current drive for viruses. To change the current drive, type the drive letter followed by a colon (example: **A:**) and then press **Enter**.

◆ The MSAV **Main Menu** appears.

Note: To check for viruses using MSAV, refer to the next page.

ANTI-VIRUS

Check the Current Drive for Viruses

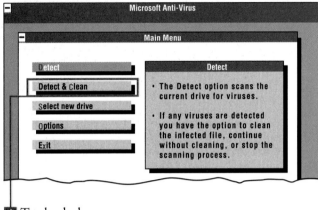

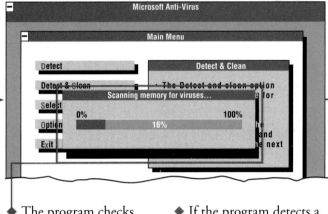

1 To check the current drive for viruses, type **C** (for Detect & **C**lean).

◆ The program checks your computer's electronic memory for viruses.

◆ If the program detects a virus, it automatically removes it.

Note: You can press **Esc** *to stop the program at any time.*

TIP ◆ You may never encounter a computer virus. In the odd chance you do, you now know how to detect and destroy it.

Exit MSAV

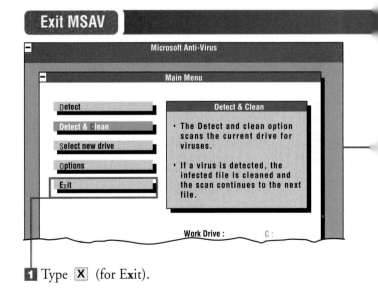

1 Type **X** (for E**x**it).

| GETTING STARTED | MANAGE DIRECTORIES | MANAGE FILES | MANAGE DISKETTES | MS-DOS SHELL | BACKUP | DATA PROTECTION | DISK MANAGEMENT |

DELETE SENTRY
ANTI-VIRUS

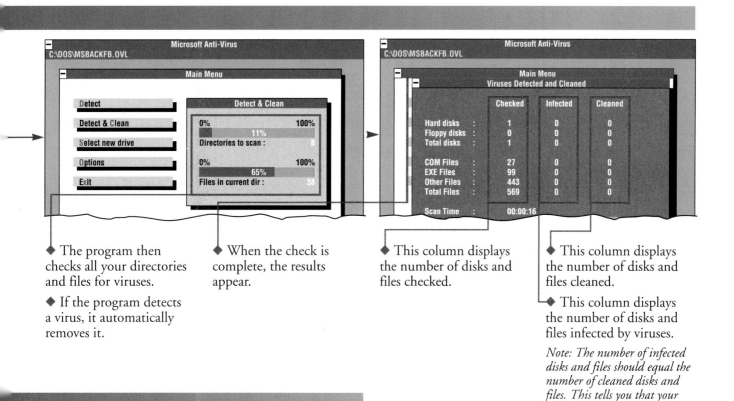

◆ The program then checks all your directories and files for viruses.

◆ If the program detects a virus, it automatically removes it.

◆ When the check is complete, the results appear.

◆ This column displays the number of disks and files checked.

◆ This column displays the number of disks and files cleaned.

◆ This column displays the number of disks and files infected by viruses.

Note: The number of infected disks and files should equal the number of cleaned disks and files. This tells you that your drive is virus free.

2 Press **Enter** to return to the **Main Menu**.

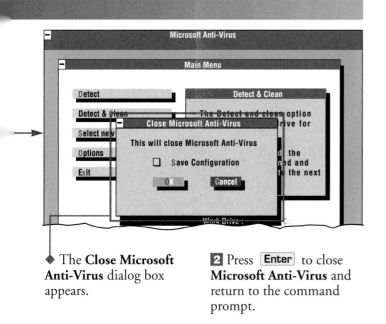

◆ The **Close Microsoft Anti-Virus** dialog box appears.

2 Press **Enter** to close **Microsoft Anti-Virus** and return to the command prompt.

CHECK DISK

The Check Disk command (typed as CHKDSK) finds and corrects problems on your hard or floppy drive. It also displays a status report of your disk.

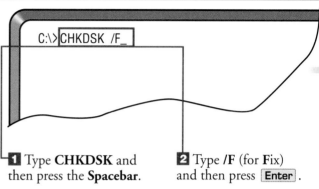

C:\> CHKDSK /F_

1 Type **CHKDSK** and then press the **Spacebar**.

2 Type **/F** (for **Fix**) and then press **Enter**.

The Check Disk command is:

CHKDSK | **DRIVE** | **/F**

DRIVE Tells MS-DOS which drive you want to check. If you omit the drive, MS-DOS checks the current drive.

/F Enables you to repair any problems encountered during the check.

WHEN SHOULD I USE THE CHECK DISK COMMAND?

Use the Check Disk command once a month. Use it immediately if:

◆ Your computer temporarily shuts down due to a power failure.

◆ You restart your computer because the screen froze.

◆ You accidentally restart your computer while running a program.

GETTING STARTED	MANAGE DIRECTORIES	MANAGE FILES	MANAGE DISKETTES	MS-DOS SHELL	BACKUP	DATA PROTECTION	DISK MANAGEMENT

CHECK DISK
DOUBLESPACE
DEFRAGMENTER

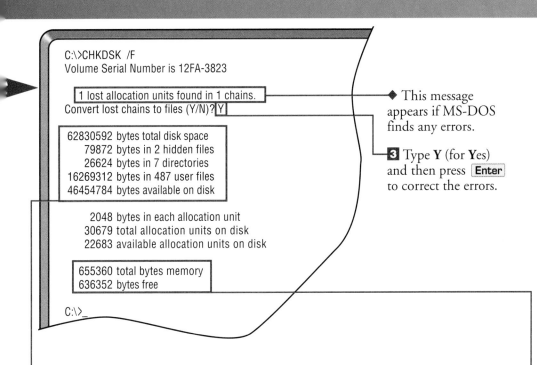

```
C:\>CHKDSK /F
Volume Serial Number is 12FA-3823

1 lost allocation units found in 1 chains.
Convert lost chains to files (Y/N)? Y

62830592 bytes total disk space
   79872 bytes in 2 hidden files
   26624 bytes in 7 directories
16269312 bytes in 487 user files
46454784 bytes available on disk

    2048 bytes in each allocation unit
   30679 total allocation units on disk
   22683 available allocation units on disk

  655360 total bytes memory
  636352 bytes free

C:\>_
```

◆ This message appears if MS-DOS finds any errors.

3 Type **Y** (for **Y**es) and then press **Enter** to correct the errors.

C:\ Root Directory

Check Disk converts any problem files to files named FILE0001.CHK, FILE0002.CHK, etc. MS-DOS stores these files in your root directory.

To increase the capacity of your hard drive, delete these files. For information on deleting files, refer to page 48.

Total disk space

The total amount of storage space on the disk.

Directories

The number of directories and the space they occupy.

Bytes available on disk

The amount of disk space still available.

Total memory

The total amount of electronic memory.

Hidden files

The number of hidden files and the space they occupy.

User files

The number of programs and data files and the space they occupy.

Bytes free

The amount of electronic memory available for running programs.

DOUBLESPACE

You can use DoubleSpace to compress the data stored on your hard drive. Your compressed drive will have 50 to 100 percent more free space.

Compression works by replacing long strings of characters with shorter strings.

For example, if "#" = "THE":

THEre THEy went to THE
(not compressed = 22 characters)

#re #y went to #
(compressed = 16 characters)

The compressed string of characters is almost 30% shorter.

You only need to install DoubleSpace once. The program then works invisibly, compressing and decompressing your data.

◆ When you store new data on your hard drive, DoubleSpace automatically compresses it to reduce the amount of disk space required.

◆ When you use data stored on your hard drive, DoubleSpace automatically decompresses it.

TIP ◆ Everyone should use DoubleSpace to increase their hard drive capacity, especially those who have computers with limited disk space (example: portable computers).

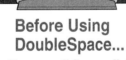

Before Using DoubleSpace...

◆ **Remove all floppy disks from your computer.**

◆ **Exit all programs.**

◆ **Run CHKDSK /F. See pages 110-111 for more information.**

◆ **Back up your data files. See pages 86-93 for more information.**

DOUBLESPACE

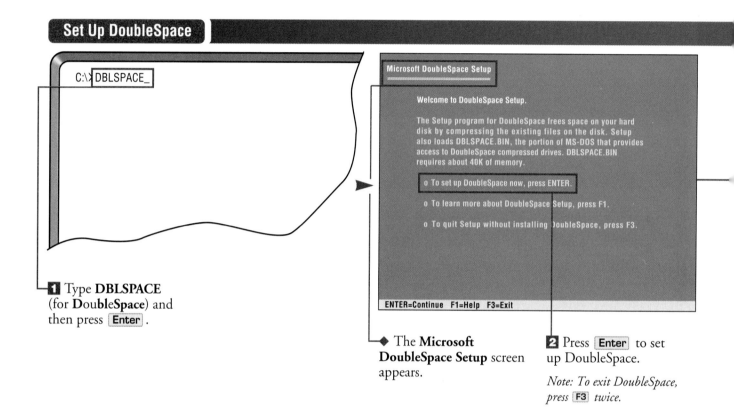

`C:\>DBLSPACE_`

1 Type **DBLSPACE** (for **DoubleSpace**) and then press **Enter**.

Microsoft DoubleSpace Setup

Welcome to DoubleSpace Setup.

The Setup program for DoubleSpace frees space on your hard disk by compressing the existing files on the disk. Setup also loads DBLSPACE.BIN, the portion of MS-DOS that provides access to DoubleSpace compressed drives. DBLSPACE.BIN requires about 40K of memory.

o To set up DoubleSpace now, press ENTER.

o To learn more about DoubleSpace Setup, press F1.

o To quit Setup without installing DoubleSpace, press F3.

ENTER=Continue   F1=Help   F3=Exit

◆ The **Microsoft DoubleSpace Setup** screen appears.

2 Press **Enter** to set up DoubleSpace.

Note: To exit DoubleSpace, press **F3** *twice.*

◆ This screen appears if you have already installed DoubleSpace.

You only need to install DoubleSpace once. To return to the MS-DOS prompt, press **Alt**, **D**, **X**.

Drive Compress Tools Help

Drive	Description	Free Space (MB)	Total Space (MB)
C	Compressed hard drive	92.59	110.15

To work with a compressed drive, press the UP ARROW or DOWN ARROW key to select it. Then, choose the action you want from the Drive or Tools menu.

To quit DoubleSpace, choose Exit from the Drive menu. For help, press F1.

DoubleSpace   F1=Help   ALT=Menu Bar   ↓=Next Item   ↑=Previous Item

GETTING STARTED	MANAGE DIRECTORIES	MANAGE FILES	MANAGE DISKETTES	MS-DOS SHELL	BACKUP	DATA PROTECTION	DISK MANAGEMENT

CHECK DISK
DOUBLESPACE
DEFRAGMENTER

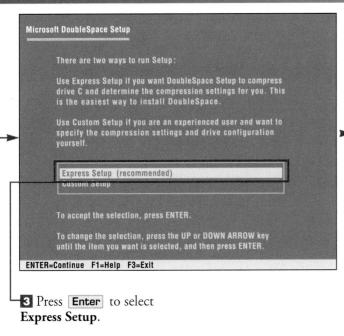

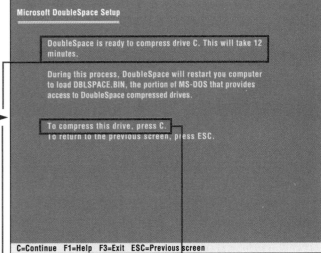

3 Press **Enter** to select **Express Setup**.

◆ DoubleSpace is ready to compress drive C. It displays the estimated time required to compress the drive (example: 12 minutes).

Note: To exit DoubleSpace, press **F3** *twice.*

4 Press **C** to compress the drive.

◆ DoubleSpace will restart your computer.

Note: Refer to the next page to continue the DoubleSpace Setup process.

DOUBLESPACE

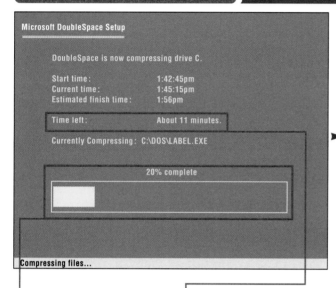

```
Microsoft DoubleSpace Setup

        DoubleSpace is now compressing drive C.

        Start time:              1:42:45pm
        Current time:            1:45:15pm
        Estimated finish time:   1:56pm

        Time left:               About 11 minutes.

        Currently Compressing:  C:\DOS\LABEL.EXE

                          20% complete


Compressing files...
```

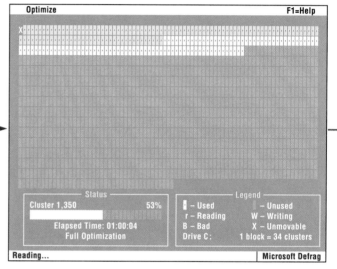

```
Optimize                                        F1=Help
X

                        ── Status ──              ── Legend ──
        Cluster 1,350               53%     ▌ – Used       ▌ – Unused
        ▌▌▌▌▌▌▌▌▌                            r – Reading    W – Writing
               Elapsed Time: 01:00:04       B – Bad        X – Unmovable
               Full Optimization            Drive C:       1 block = 34 clusters
Reading...                                             Microsoft Defrag
```

◆ This indicates the percentage of data on your hard drive compressed by DoubleSpace.

◆ This indicates the estimated time left.

◆ When DoubleSpace finishes compressing your hard drive, it defragments your files.

◆ The defragmenting process reorganizes the files stored on your hard drive to optimize disk performance.

DoubleSpace compresses the data on your hard drive to increase its storage capacity.

DoubleSpace then defragments your hard drive to improve its efficiency.

Note: For more information on defragmenting your hard drive, refer to page 118.

CHECK DISK
DOUBLESPACE
DEFRAGMENTER

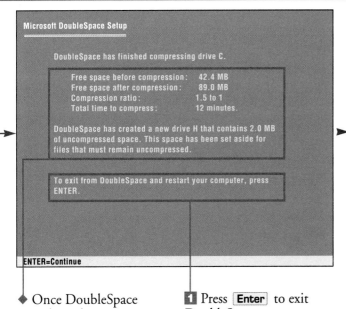

Microsoft DoubleSpace Setup

DoubleSpace has finished compressing drive C.

Free space before compression: 42.4 MB
Free space after compression: 89.0 MB
Compression ratio: 1.5 to 1
Total time to compress: 12 minutes.

DoubleSpace has created a new drive H that contains 2.0 MB of uncompressed space. This space has been set aside for files that must remain uncompressed.

To exit from DoubleSpace and restart your computer, press ENTER.

ENTER=Continue

Microsoft DoubleSpace Setup

DoubleSpace is making final modifications to your AUTOEXEC.BAT and CONFIG.SYS files, and will then restart your computer to enable the compressed drive.

Preparing final DBLSPACE.INI file...

◆ Once DoubleSpace completes the defragmenting process, it displays information about your compressed drive.

1 Press **Enter** to exit DoubleSpace.

◆ DoubleSpace makes some final changes and then restarts your computer.

◆ You may now use your hard drive as usual.

◆ Your compressed drive will have 50 to 100 percent more free space.

DEFRAGMENTER

HOW MS-DOS STORES YOUR FILES

Inside the case of your hard drive is a stack of platters called disks. These disks magnetically store your data files.

When you save a file to your hard drive, MS-DOS stores it in one or more storage spaces called "clusters." MS-DOS tries to keep together all the clusters of a file by placing them in adjacent spaces. This way, your computer can retrieve a file quickly and efficiently.

◆ cluster

◆ one file

Eventually, you will delete files from your hard drive. This leaves empty spaces between the remaining files.

WHY DO FILES FRAGMENT?

Sometimes, MS-DOS cannot find enough adjacent empty spaces to store an entire file. It must then break the file apart and store the fragments in empty spaces all over the disk. This process is called disk fragmentation.

Note: Files may also fragment when you add additional information to them.

Before and After Defragmenting

BEFORE DEFRAGMENTING

A fragmented disk contains files that are broken up and scattered around it. When MS-DOS wants to retrieve a file, it must search the entire disk to find all the fragments of that file.

Fragmentation does not alter the information stored on your hard drive, but it does reduce performance speed.

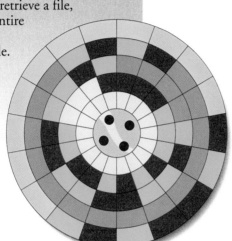

AFTER DEFRAGMENTING

Defragmenter places all the clusters of each file together. This reduces the time your hard drive requires to retrieve a file.

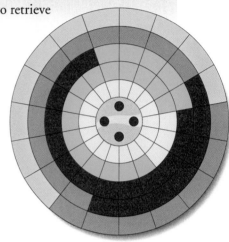

Sort Files During Defragmentation

When you defragment the files on your hard drive, you can also sort them by name, extension, date or size (in ascending or descending order). This can make it easier for you to find your data files.

Note: Any new files you add to the computer after using the Defragmenter will not appear "sorted."

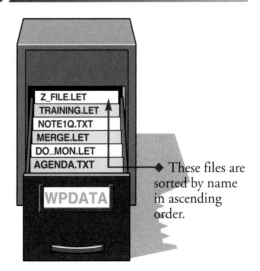

Z_FILE.LET
TRAINING.LET
NOTE1Q.TXT
MERGE.LET
DO_MON.LET
AGENDA.TXT

WPDATA

◆ These files are sorted by name in ascending order.

DEFRAGMENTER

Defragment Files on Your Hard Drive (C:)

IMPORTANT!

◆ Use Defragmenter at least twice a month.

◆ Do not turn off or reset your computer while running Defragmenter.

◆ Before using Defragmenter:

➤ Exit all programs, including Windows.

➤ Run **CHKDSK /F** described on page 110.

DEFRAGMENT WITHOUT SORTING FILES

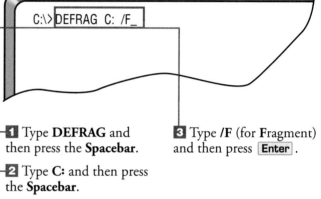

1 Type **DEFRAG** and then press the **Spacebar**.

2 Type **C:** and then press the **Spacebar**.

3 Type **/F** (for **F**ragment) and then press `Enter`.

DEFRAGMENT AND SORT FILES BY NAME (A TO Z)

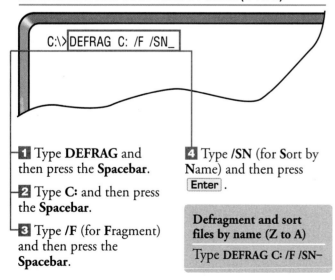

1 Type **DEFRAG** and then press the **Spacebar**.

2 Type **C:** and then press the **Spacebar**.

3 Type **/F** (for **F**ragment) and then press the **Spacebar**.

4 Type **/SN** (for **S**ort by **N**ame) and then press `Enter`.

> **Defragment and sort files by name (Z to A)**
>
> Type **DEFRAG C: /F /SN–**

DEFRAGMENT AND SORT FILES BY EXTENSION (A TO Z)

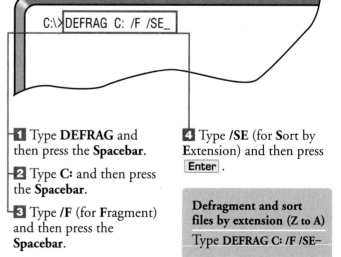

1 Type **DEFRAG** and then press the **Spacebar**.

2 Type **C:** and then press the **Spacebar**.

3 Type **/F** (for **F**ragment) and then press the **Spacebar**.

4 Type **/SE** (for **S**ort by **E**xtension) and then press `Enter`.

> **Defragment and sort files by extension (Z to A)**
>
> Type **DEFRAG C: /F /SE–**

CHECK DISK
DOUBLESPACE
DEFRAGMENTER

DEFRAGMENT AND SORT FILES BY DATE (EARLIEST FIRST)

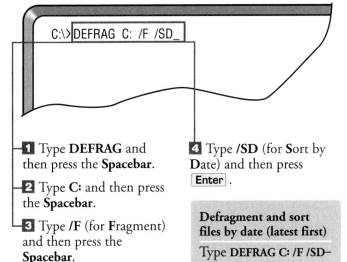

C:\> DEFRAG C: /F /SD_

1 Type **DEFRAG** and then press the **Spacebar**.

2 Type **C:** and then press the **Spacebar**.

3 Type **/F** (for **F**ragment) and then press the **Spacebar**.

4 Type **/SD** (for **S**ort by **D**ate) and then press Enter.

Defragment and sort files by date (latest first)

Type **DEFRAG C: /F /SD–**

DEFRAGMENT AND SORT FILES BY SIZE (SMALLEST FIRST)

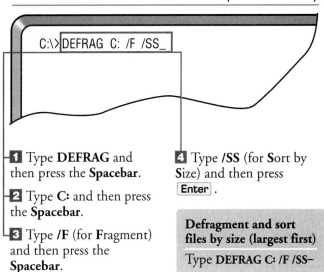

C:\> DEFRAG C: /F /SS_

1 Type **DEFRAG** and then press the **Spacebar**.

2 Type **C:** and then press the **Spacebar**.

3 Type **/F** (for **F**ragment) and then press the **Spacebar**.

4 Type **/SS** (for **S**ort by **S**ize) and then press Enter.

Defragment and sort files by size (largest first)

Type **DEFRAG C: /F /SS–**

Defragmenter reorganizes the files stored on your hard drive to optimize disk performance.

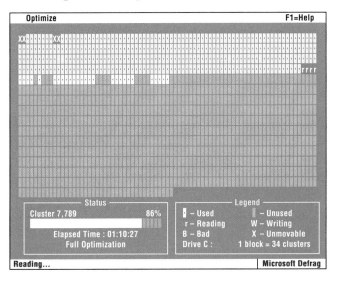

If you install DoubleSpace before running Defragmenter, this screen appears.

```
Please wait
Now starting the DoubleSpace program
to defragment your compressed drive
DoubleSpace is defragmenting drive C...
DoubleSpace is remounting drive C.
DoubleSpace has finished defragmenting drive C.

C:\>_
```

121

INDEX

MS-DOS Shell

Congratulations.

Look on the back cover for more of our books.